Great Christian Hymn Writers

Great Christian Hymn Writers

Jane Stuart Smith
and
Betty Carlson

CROSSWAY BOOKS • WHEATON, ILLINOIS
A DIVISION OF GOOD NEWS PUBLISHERS

Cover design: Cindy Kiple

Cover illustration: Robert Doares

First printing, 1997

Printed in the United States of America

Library of Congress Cataloging-in-Publication Data
Smith, Jane Stuart.
    Great Christian hymn writers / Jane Stuart Smith, Betty
Carlson.
        p.   cm.
    Includes bibliographical references and index.
    ISBN 0-89107-944-0
    1. Hymn writers—Biography. I. Carlson, Betty. II. Title.
BV325.S65 1997
264'.23'0922—dc21   97-15861

07	06	05	04							
15	14	13	12	11	10	9	8	7	6	5

Contents

Foreword

My dear friends, Jane Stuart Smith and Betty Carlson, have written an important book for our day. It is refreshing to learn about those who wrote poetry and music so wonderfully, so powerfully that their hymns have been sung by thousands upon thousands of men, women, and children—hearts bursting with fervor of praise to God, sorrow for sins and mistakes, pathos of deep understanding of the wonder of what Christ did, satisfaction of being able to find words and music to express what they felt—words that seem to come naturally at times out of people's own need for these words—even though coming from someone else's mind and heart a hundred years ago (more or less).

That is a long sentence, but it all *belongs* in one sentence! This much-needed book gives *us* knowledge and understanding of the men and women whose wisdom is a part of the life of a succession of individuals and families. Generations of people, in their church worship, singing around the piano in family times, at camps, in youth groups, or in old folk's homes, have felt these hymns belong to them.

In telling about the lives of these gifted writers, this book makes them real to us. However, in reading, one also becomes more eager to sing the fine old hymns again, and one looks forward to meeting these people in heaven. We become richer for having another glimpse of the wonder of human minds, made creative, made to have ideas and to choose among those ideas. We worship the Creator who made human beings, man and woman, in His image that they may be creative.

One also becomes aware of the creativity of Jane and Betty, whose minds were full of the ideas brought forth in the book as they looked out over the fields and mountains in front of their dear Chalet le Chesalet—the same mountains that inspired Frances Ridley Havergal in Champery to write some of her hymns. I like to think of Frances Havergal's prayers being answered in the existence of L'Abri, answered as she prayed for that area of the world, so many years ago. But prayers were also answered in the persistence and work, with patience in research, by Jane and Betty these many years later to bring us an ease of discovery (without the hard work) as we sit reading in our gardens or by our fireplaces.

—*Edith Schaeffer*

Prelude

Speak to one another with psalms,
hymns and spiritual songs. Sing and
make music in your heart to the Lord.

EPHESIANS 5:19

It has been said that the Christian church started on its way singing—because the Christian faith is a singing faith. The great religious revivals have been profoundly influenced by music. Not only was the Gospel preached, but it was also sung into the hearts of the people by men such as Ambrose, Huss, Luther, Zinzendorf, Wesley, Moody. Where a renewed spiritual life occurs, one finds the richest period of hymn singing and hymn writing. One might say that "a spiritual church is a singing church."

A great outburst of singing follows every fresh work of the Spirit, every time of revival in the church. It is said of the Wesleys that for every person they won with their preaching, ten persons were won through their music.

Often people who do not write poetry and music assume that lyrics and melodies flow easily and readily out of the minds of creative individuals. But the poet Tennyson said, "A good hymn is the most difficult thing in the world to write." There are times, however, when something will happen to cause the words simply to pour forth.

One of those times came for Charles Wesley at a point when he was deeply burdened by certain spiritual problems. He was in his study when suddenly through the open window he saw a small bird pursued by a large hawk. Through the window fluttered the frightened sparrow—into Wesley's arms. Out of this unusual experience he wrote:

> *Jesus, lover of my soul,*
> *Let me to Thy bosom fly,*
> *While the nearer waters roll,*
> *While the tempest still is high.*
> *Hide me, O my Savior, hide,*
> *Till the storm of life is past;*
> *Safe into the haven guide,*
> *O receive my soul at last!*

Nearly every good hymn has a story behind it, a story worth knowing about, and that is why we have written this book. I think of how many times in my life I have sung "Joy to the World," "Our God, Our Help in Ages Past," and "When I Survey the Wondrous Cross" without knowing that Isaac Watts was the author of all three. And even more interesting, he was the one in England to open the door to the singing of hymns. As Elsie Houghton, author of *Christian Hymn Writers*, said, "All later hymn writers, even when they excel him, are his debtors."

It is helpful to know who wrote our hymns. It enables us to sing praises with deeper appreciation and enthusiasm to our living God.

Introduction

People do not have to be musicians in order to sing hymns. The word, *hymn*, means "song of praise." These songs of praise are the way most Christians are introduced to music in churches or at home. Many individuals would probably never sing if it were not for hymns. If Larry Snyder, a member of L'Abri Fellowship in Switzerland, should happen to stand next to Jane or me in church, he would always whisper, "Now remember, I can't sing, but I love hymns, so I'm going to monotone away!"

I don't think what I do is exactly singing either, but Larry and I felt we were singing, particularly if we had the backing of Jane's rich, full sounds. It is good for all of us to sing our praise to the Lord, and it is healthy.

Luther, the father of evangelical hymnody, said, "Next to the Word of God, the noble art of music is the greatest treasure in this world." And Francis Schaeffer expressed it this way: "A wonderful companion to the Bible is a good hymnbook." The study of hymns utilizes the Bible, poetry, literature, biography, music, and church history. Indeed, hymnology contains a wealth of valuable and challenging information to enrich our spiritual lives. For this reason we felt compelled to write this small volume, hoping it might open the door to a deeper appreciation of the wonder of hymns.

It is true that the minister in the pulpit has the responsibility to instruct his people, but men and women with their God-given gifts also "speak" in churches through their hymns that bring inspiration and comfort to countless multitudes. As Luther, who restored congregational singing in the churches, said, "Our Lord speaks with us through His holy Word, and we in return speak with Him through prayer and songs of praise. Hymns are essentially the congregation's part in a worship service."

I had sung the hymn "Have Thine Own Way, Lord" for many years without thinking about who wrote it or why. Now that I know something about Adelaide Pollard and why she wrote this hymn, my appreciation of the message she has passed on to us has greatly increased. I find this hymn a very useful prayer when wondering, as we all do sometimes, what is next in life.

> *Have Thine own way, Lord!*
> *Have Thine own way!*
> *Hold o'er my being absolute sway!*
> *Fill with Thy Spirit till all shall see*
> *Christ, only, always living in me!*

1

Sarah Flower Adams
1805–1848

Music hath charms
to soothe the savage beast,
to soften rocks,
or bend a knotted oak.

WILLIAM CONGREVE

Nearer, My God, to Thee" was the favorite hymn of William McKinley, the third president of the United States to be assassinated. As he was dying, he whispered softly, "Nearer, my God, to Thee, nearer to Thee, e'en though it be a cross that raiseth me." He told the doctor who attended him, "This has been my constant prayer."

The writer of this beloved hymn, Sarah Flower Adams, was born in Great Harlow, England, in 1805. Her father was the editor of the *Cambridge Intelligence*. When Sarah was only five, her mother died.

Even though Sarah was a talented poet, her dream was to be an actress. She believed that moral truths could be taught from the stage as well as from the pulpit, but she was never able to achieve her goal because of uncertain health. Thus she turned her talents to writing.

It has been said that the great English poet Robert Browning indirectly inspired Mrs. Adams's hymn. Their friendship began when they were children. A few years later her faith seemed to waver because of the fatigue and annoyance of ill health. It is thought that the influence of Browning revived and confirmed her Christian faith, making it possible for her to write "Nearer, My God, to Thee."

The hymn is based on Genesis 28:11–17. When Jacob flees from Esau, he dreams of a ladder reaching up to heaven. Sarah Flower Adams expressed in her hymn the truth that even in darkness and trouble, we may be lifted nearer to God. Many Christians will add, *particularly* in troubled and dark moments the comforting presence of Christ is real.

In 1834 Sarah married William Adams, an engineer, and moved to London. Although she was influenced by Unitarianism, she became a Baptist near the end of her life. Her hymns do indicate that she had a living faith in the Lord Jesus Christ.

Her health continued to be poor. When she began to care for her sister Eliza, she grew more and more fragile. She died two years after her sister, in 1848.

In her lifetime "Nearer, My God, to Thee" appeared in a small, provincial hymnbook, but she had no idea that it would become a part of universal hymnody and a favorite of countless numbers of people, including Queen Victoria and Edward VII. At the time of President William McKinley's funeral, "Nearer, My God, to Thee" was sung in churches all over America.

In 1912 the ocean liner *Titanic* struck an iceberg about 1,600 miles northeast of New York City on its first voyage from England to the U.S.A. Less than half of the 2,200 persons aboard, mostly women and children, were able to find room in the lifeboats. In the final moments as the ship slowly sank beneath the waves, its band played "Nearer, My God, to Thee."

When Sarah Adams put down these deep, personal thoughts to comfort and uplift her own heart, she did not realize she would be speaking to a far wider audience someday, that her hymn would be sung wherever Christians gather.

> *Nearer, my God, to Thee,*
> *Nearer to Thee!*
> *E'en though it be a cross*
> *That raiseth me;*
> *Still all my song shall be,*
> *Nearer, my God, to Thee,*
> *Nearer, my God, to Thee,*
> *Nearer to Thee!*

2

Joseph Addison
1672–1719

Through all eternity to Thee
A joyful song I'll raise;
But oh, eternity's too short
To utter all Thy praise!

JOSEPH ADDISON

One of the great literary geniuses of England, Joseph Addison had planned to follow in the footsteps of his clergyman father. But while he studied at Magdalen College, Oxford, he excelled in literary studies and was especially skilled in writing Latin verse. He began to be interested in two other careers—writing and diplomatic service.

In order to gain knowledge of foreign courts as well as ideas for writing, he went to Italy on a traveling scholarship in 1700. From there he moved on to Switzerland, to Vienna and Germany, and finally to the Netherlands, returning to England upon the death of his father.

In 1704 a French and Bavarian army threatened the city of Vienna. Although they were outnumbered, England and its allies surprised the French at Blenheim. The Duke of Marlborough captured the French commander and 13,000 of the Franco-Bavarian troops. It was the first major French defeat in fifty years.

To celebrate the victory, Joseph Addison wrote the poem, "The Campaign." The poem gained immediate success and was such an aid to the Whig party that Addison was appointed undersecretary of state in 1706 and secretary of state in 1717 under George I. From 1708 until his death, Addison had a seat in Parliament. No other individual, relying on literary talent alone, has risen so high in state affairs.

Addison is perhaps best known for his essays, which appeared in *The Tatler* and later in *The Spectator*—famous newspapers in the day of Queen Anne. Written in collaboration with Richard Steele, Addison's classmate and lifelong friend, these writings became the model for polished, elegant English until the end of the eighteenth century. As one critic said, "Most newspaper work is forgotten with the setting sun, but not these essays . . ." "Whosoever wishes to attain an English style," wrote Samuel Johnson, "familiar but not coarse, and elegant but not ostentatious, must give his days and nights to the study of Addison." Addison himself believed that artistry and excellence of subject matter were imperative.

The Spectator stood for reason and moderation in an age of bitter party strife. Through its pages Addison had a major influence on English public opinion in the eighteenth century. He wanted to improve the manners and morals of his time, and his pen helped make virtue the fashion. One of the most famous characters Addison and Steele invented for that purpose was Sir Roger de Coverley, a delightful country squire.

Those who knew Joseph Addison remembered his kindliness

and integrity. The charm and humor of his essays reflect his personality and illustrate the truth that if one smiles into the mirror of the world, it will answer with a smile.

Sometimes Addison appended a poem to one of his essays. From this source came five hymns of rare beauty. They are called the Creation Hymns—"The Spacious Firmament on High," "How Are Thy Servants Blest, O Lord," "The Lord My Pasture Shall Prepare," "When Rising from the Bed of Death," and "When All Thy Mercies, O My God." In the essay introducing this last hymn, Addison wrote, "Any blessing which we enjoy, by what means soever derived, is the gift of Him who is the great Author of good and the Father of mercies."

Joseph Addison was a devout Christian, and even when he was dying, he was not praying for himself, but for his brother-in-law, the Earl of Warwick, who was not a believer. Addison asked the one taking care of him to allow the earl to come to his bedside, and in a most gentle and modest way he said, "See in what peace a Christian can die!" Addison is buried in Westminster Abbey.

When all Thy mercies, O my God,
My rising soul surveys,
Transported with the view, I'm lost
In wonder, love, and praise.

3

Cecil Frances Alexander
1823–1895

*Jesus said, "Let the
little children come to me,
and do not hinder them,
for the kingdom of heaven
belongs to such as these."*

MATTHEW 19:14

Cecil Frances Alexander began writing poetry at the age of nine. Fearing that her father, a stern military officer, would disapprove, she hid the poems under the carpet in her bedroom. But one day, he discovered them. To her surprise and delight, he gave her a box, with a large slit in the top, for her poems. On Saturday evenings, he opened the box and brought out the new poems, read them aloud, and made helpful and encouraging comments.

Cecil knew that children loved poetry and could memorize the great truths of the Bible quickly. Many of her poems were written to help make the Scripture more understandable to them. In fact, almost all of her four hundred hymns and poems were for children. The language is simple and clear, but not childish or sentimental. Her poems set forth some of the most profound truths of the Christian faith and are loved by adults also. Many are based on the church catechism and the Apostles' Creed.

Some of her best poems and hymns were written before she was twenty. At age twenty-five, she published a volume of these hymns for children that has probably never been equaled.

In 1850 she married William Alexander, a parish minister who later became a Bishop and then Archbishop of Ireland. In the early years of their marriage, they served a church in an impoverished rural area. Cecil did not just sit back and write poetry and weep for the needs of her poor neighbors. In *The Story of Christian Hymnody*, E. E. Ryden tells how she expressed her concern: "From one poor house to another, from one bed of sickness to another, from one sorrow to another, she went. Christ was ever with her and in her, and all felt her influence." Later she gave the profits from her hymnbook to support handicapped children in the north of Ireland.

Shortly before Archbishop Alexander died, he remarked that he would be remembered chiefly as the husband of the woman who wrote "There Is a Green Hill Far Away" and several other beloved hymns. One of her poems, "The Burial of Moses," is considered one of the finest of its kind in the English language.

Her husband was right. Although he occupied an important position in the church, few people today remember his name. People might not know his wife's name, but they know and love her hymns.

Cecil's other outstanding hymns are the Christmas carol "Once in Royal David's City" and "All Things Bright and

Beautiful," which is based on the phrase "Maker of heaven and earth" in the Apostles' Creed. These two hymns, along with "There Is a Green Hill Far Away," will be sung as long as the church on earth respects the Bible and sings praise to the triune God.

Mrs. Alexander also wrote "Jesus Calls Us O'er the Tumult," based on the call of Andrew to serve the Lord. The words speak to and for all of us when overcome by the troubles and hardships of life.

Cecil Frances Alexander died at the age of seventy-two and is buried in the Londonderry Cathedral in Ireland. When her husband died sixteen years later, the congregation sang at his funeral "There Is a Green Hill Far Away." The great French composer, Charles Gounod, considered this a near perfect hymn, with simplicity its greatest beauty.

> *There is a green hill far away,*
> *Without a city wall,*
> *Where the dear Lord was crucified,*
> *Who died to save us all.*

In this century, James Herriot, a country veterinarian, used words from the refrain of Mrs. Alexander's hymn, "All Things Bright and Beautiful" as the titles to his four very popular books. Throughout his career, he kept detailed diaries which enabled him to tell with freshness the quaint, humorous, sometimes sad stories of his life caring for animals and people. His first book, *All Creatures Great and Small*, was recognized immediately as a classic.

Each little flow'r that opens,
Each little bird that sings,
He made their glowing colors,
He made their tiny wings.
Yes, all things bright and beautiful,
All creatures great and small,
All things wise and wonderful,
The Lord God made them all.

4

Henry Alford
1810–1871

Come, ye thankful people, come,
Raise the song of harvest home.

HENRY ALFORD

Henry Alford, the great English New Testament scholar and dean of Canterbury, seemed to have a perpetual spirit of gratitude. At the end of a day, whether good or bad, and after every meal he would stand up and give thanks to God for blessing him so richly. It was Alford who wrote the great harvest-thanksgiving hymn, "Come, Ye Thankful People, Come."

Henry Alford was born in London, the son of an Anglican clergyman. After graduating from Cambridge, Henry became curate to his father and rose rapidly to other positions, until he became the dean of Canterbury.

Alford was a multitalented man—a musician, painter, wood carver, preacher, teacher, scholar, and poet. The major work of his life was his Greek Testament, on which he labored for twenty years. Uniting fresh treatment with wide learning, it introduced

German New Testament scholarship to English readers. Through this work Alford made a notable contribution to biblical knowledge on both sides of the Atlantic. He also edited the writings of John Donne, another great Christian writer.

Because of his strenuous life and countless activities in the Christian ministry, he suffered a physical breakdown at the age of sixty-one. He died in 1871. At the funeral in Canterbury Cathedral, the congregation sang another of his hymns, "Ten Thousand Times Ten Thousand," with great feeling.

> *Ten thousand times ten thousand*
> *In sparkling raiment bright,*
> *The armies of the ransomed saints*
> *Throng up the steeps of light:*
> *'Tis finished, all is finished,*
> *Their fight with death and sin:*
> *Fling open wide the golden gates,*
> *And let the victors in.*

5

Ambrose of Milan
340–397

Praise to God the Father sing,
Praise to God the Son, our King,
Praise to God the Spirit be
Ever and eternally.

AURELIUS AMBROSE

It was Ambrose who in the fourth century made hymns popular. Troubled that in the mass one individual sang all the psalms and hymns while the congregation merely listened, he introduced antiphonal singing, which allowed the congregation to sing alternating parts of the music. He also "bewitched" the populace with his hymns and a new form of chant based on Eastern melodies. People loved the simple rhythms and joyous tunes. Called the Father of Latin Hymnody, Ambrose not only wrote hymns himself, but also encouraged others to do so.

Born into a rich aristocratic family, he grew up in Rome and studied to be a lawyer. He served so well as a provincial governor that the Catholic laity demanded that he be appointed the next Bishop of Milan. In eight days his status changed from unbaptized layman to bishop of the church.

Ambrose sold all his possessions and entered into his church duties with fervor. He became one of the most famous bishops of all time. Adviser to three Roman emperors, he established the medieval concept of a Christian emperor serving under orders from Christ and so subject to the advice of his bishop. The relations Ambrose had with Emperor Theodosius I provided a model for church/state relations in the Middle Ages.

Ambrose defended the doctrine of the Trinity against the heresy of the Arians, who believed that only God the Father was completely divine. Empress Justina, who favored the Arians, tried to make Ambrose open his churches to the Arians. But he insisted that the state had no right to interfere in matters of doctrine.

Angered, Justina sent soldiers to the new basilica in Milan to enforce her decree; however, the people rallied around their beloved bishop. When the soldiers arrived, they found the congregation praying and singing in the church. The scene made such an impression on the soldiers that they too joined in the joyous singing.

On Easter Sunday in 387, Ambrose baptized his most famous convert—Augustine, the great Christian theologian. According to Augustine, the hymns and preaching of Ambrose had made a profound impression on his soul. Tradition has it that during the baptism, the two improvised the "Te Deum Laudamus" (We Praise Thee, O God) in alternate verses. This may well be true, since it was the practice of the early church to create hymns when inspired by strong religious feeling.

Ambrose was one of the most influential people of his time—a great scholar, organizer, statesman, and theologian. He was a man of strong character and a model bishop. His sermons are acclaimed as masterpieces of Latin eloquence. In Milan today his feast day, December 7, is still celebrated.

After his death congregational singing gradually declined, and Gregorian chant was confined to the choir and priests. Fortunately, the Holy Spirit moved mightily in the Reformation, and at Luther's insistence, singing returned to a central place in worship. Luther prized Ambrose's hymns enough to translate and include "Savior of the Nations, Come" in his first hymnbook in 1524.

> *Savior of the nations, come,*
> *Virgin's Son, make here Thy home;*
> *Marvel now, O heav'n and earth,*
> *That the Lord chose such a birth.*

6

Katherine Lee Bates
1859–1929

To a poet nothing can be useless.

SAMUEL JOHNSON

How many times have I driven across the midwestern states on the way to Colorado and stopped to stare at the beauty of the corn or wheat fields spread out for miles—then the growing excitement of coming into rolling hills, followed by the awe of seeing the mountains framed by a sunset! Not being a poet, I have never recorded any of this. How thankful I am that Katherine Lee Bates captured all of it so well in the great patriotic hymn, "America the Beautiful."

Miss Bates was the daughter of a Congregational clergyman in Falmouth, Massachusetts. Professor of English literature at Wellesley College and later distinguished head of the English department there, Katherine was the author or editor of more than twenty works.

One summer she traveled with some friends from Massachusetts to Colorado. They stopped in Chicago at the Columbian Exposition of 1893. The beauty of the "White City" impressed her and became part of the last stanza of her hymn, "Thine alabaster cities gleam, undimmed by human tears!"

What she saw on this memorable trip aroused deep feelings in her heart. They stood atop Pike's Peak and watched the sun rise, fingers of light expanding across the world below. The next evening, they talked about what they had seen. They all were impressed with the greatness, the vastness of America, but Katherine understood something more. She said, "Greatness and goodness are not necessarily synonymous. Rome was great, but she was not good, and for that reason the Roman Empire fell . . . The Spanish Empire was a great one also, but as morally rotten as the Roman; consequently the Spanish Empire is no more. Unless we are willing to crown our greatness with goodness, and our bounty with brotherhood, our beloved America may go the same way" (*The Story of Christian Hymnody* by E. E. Ryden, page 592).

After this long, strenuous, exciting day, the friends said good night, and Katherine went to bed. But she could not sleep. Instead she wrote these words:

> *O beautiful for spacious skies,*
> *For amber waves of grain,*
> *For purple mountain majesties,*
> *Above the fruited plain!*

As she began to form the verses, she ended each one with a prayer to God to mend the flaws of America, to refine its gold, and to crown its good with brotherhood "from sea to shining sea."

This patriotic hymn is a reminder of America's noble past, a vivid picture of the Pilgrims whose struggles paved the way for freedom and of our need today to match our national greatness with godly living.

When Katherine finished her poem, she put it in her notebook, and there it remained for two years. Then in 1895 she decided to send it to a Boston publisher.

It was published the same year, and perhaps no other hymn caught on so quickly with the public. She was thrilled.

Dissatisfied with the words as originally written, Katherine submitted a revised version in 1904. It is this version which is sung today, usually to the tune "Materna" written by Samuel Augustus Ward.

> *America! America!*
> *God shed His grace on thee,*
> *And crown thy good with brotherhood*
> *From sea to shining sea.*

7

Bernard of Clairvaux
1090–1153

Thy truth unchanged hath ever stood,
Thou savest those that on Thee call;
To them that seek Thee, Thou art good,
To them that find Thee, all in all.

BERNARD OF CLAIRVAUX

Illness plagued Bernard of Clairvaux for most of his life, but as his health worsened, his spirituality deepened. He lived as an ascetic, yet he led a very busy life which reduced him almost to a skeleton. However, nothing dampened his zeal.

Bernard was born into a noble family near Dijon, France. His father was a Burgundian knight. With all the advantages of high birth, Bernard had graceful manners and great eloquence, and he was handsome. Both his parents modeled a high standard of behavior for the young boy. His mother taught him the Christian faith, and he grew up loving the Lord. Because of her influence, he entered a monastery after her death, bringing along twelve companions, including an uncle and several brothers.

When only twenty-four, he founded a monastery that eventually grew famous. He called it Clara Vallis, or "Beautiful

Valley," which became "Clairvaux." Bandits terrorized the valley during construction of the monastery, and Bernard and his companions nearly starved in the process.

Though there were always pressing claims on his time, the Abbot Bernard regularly devoted part of his schedule to study, particularly of the Bible. His knowledge of Scripture was remarkable, so that he became one of the most influential religious men in Europe. Gifted with extraordinary eloquence and spiritual fervor, he preached with results that were almost miraculous. He had many pupils who went on to wield great influence in the Roman Catholic church. Even kings and spiritual dignitaries sought his counsel.

Throughout the ages Bernard's mystical poetry has given comfort and inspiration. The famous Scottish missionary to Africa, David Livingstone, said, "That hymn of St. Bernard on the name of Jesus . . . rings in my ears as I wander across the wide, wide wilderness."

Bernard is considered today one of the most prominent personalities of the twelfth century, even of the entire Middle Ages, and of church history in general. Three hundred years after Bernard's death Luther wrote, "Bernard was the best monk that ever lived, whom I love beyond all the rest put together."

Undoubtedly, Luther also loved Bernard's three magnificent hymns—"Jesus, the Very Thought of Thee," "Jesus, Thou Joy of Loving Hearts," and "O Sacred Head, Now Wounded." This last sublime hymn had another admirer. It might well be considered the theme song of Johann Sebastian Bach.

Bernard represented the best and purest of monastic life in his time. His monks loved him as their father. He was in the true evangelical succession and followed the doctrine of Augustine. He delighted to share with all people that Christ is the sinner's only hope and salvation. In the darkness of spiritual decay and moral depravity of the Middle Ages, this pious monk's wholesome life shone like a bright star.

> *Jesus, the very thought of Thee*
> *With sweetness fills my breast;*
> *But sweeter far Thy face to see*
> *And in Thy presence rest.*

8

Horatius Bonar
1808–1889

*I try to fill my hymns with the
love and light of Christ.*

HORATIUS BONAR

Although his father was a lawyer, Horatius Bonar was born into a family boasting a long line of prominent Scottish ministers. Bonar's parents encouraged their three sons to become ministers. After Horatius completed his studies at the University of Edinburgh, he began doing mission work in one of the poorest districts of the city. He noticed that the children did not enjoy singing the paraphrased psalms, so he began writing hymns with the happy tunes they liked. Though many of his hymns were written for children, they are spiritually profound and also reach the hearts of adults. During this time he wrote his first hymn for adults. Titled "Go, Labor On! Spend and Be Spent," the hymn was meant to encourage those working with him among the poor.

After four years of working in the most squalid parts of

Edinburgh, Bonar was ordained a minister of the Church of Scotland. His first sermon was on prayer, a topic especially dear to his heart. Bonar was a great man of prayer. One day a young servant of his heard him praying in his study. *If he needs to pray so much*, she thought, *what will become of me if I do not pray?* She decided to put her trust too in Jesus, the Son of God.

In his hymns Bonar always pointed to Christ as the all-sufficient Savior and to God's willingness to accept each person who comes to Him through Christ. Bonar had a special gift for listening and helping those who thought their sins too grievous to be forgiven. One of these, a young man in deep despair, was convinced his case was hopeless. Bonar assured him that God, through the shed blood of Jesus Christ, was willing to forgive him. But the unhappy man could not seem to grasp this truth.

Bonar suddenly said, "Tell me, which is of greater weight in the eyes of God—your sin, black as it is, or the blood of Jesus shed for sinners?"

A light came into the eyes of the young man. He responded, "Oh, I'm sure the blood of Jesus weighs more heavily in God's sight than even my sin!" And at that moment, peace came into his heart.*

Dr. Bonar married Jane Lundie in 1843, and for forty years they shared both joy and sorrow. Five of their children died, and Bonar himself was sorely afflicted during the last two years of his life. But God used the sorrow to enrich and mellow his life. Bonar did not lose his gentle, sympathetic nature.

Dr. Horatius Bonar is recognized as one of Scotland's most eminent preachers. The basic message of his sermons was "you must be born again," and many were converted through his ministry. A great evangelical revival swept over Scotland in which Bonar and his brothers and a fellow student of Horatius from the University of Edinburgh, the saintly Robert Murray McCheyne, were involved.

Horatius Bonar was a man of great energy, and when he was not preaching, he was writing hymns and tracts. Scotland's greatest hymn writer, he wrote around six hundred hymns, some of which are still sung today. Some favorites are "I Heard the Voice of Jesus Say," "I Hear the Words of Love," "Not What These Hands Have Done," and "Here, O Lord, We See Thee Face to Face." When Bonar died in 1889, he was mourned by Christians throughout the world.

> *I heard the voice of Jesus say,*
> *"Come unto Me and rest;*
> *Lay down, thou weary one, lay down*
> *Thy head upon My breast."*
> *I came to Jesus as I was,*
> *Weary, and worn, and sad;*
> *I found in Him a resting place,*
> *And He has made me glad.*

---

*From E. E. Ryden, *The Story of Christian Hymnody* (Rock Island, IL: Augustana Press, 1959).

9

Jane L. Borthwick
1813–1897

Sarah Borthwick Findlater
1823–1907

Two are better than one.

ECCLESIASTES 4:9

The two sisters, Jane and Sarah Borthwick, along with Catherine Winkworth, gave to the English-speaking world some of the finest gems in German hymnody. Born in Edinburgh, the sisters were members of an old Scottish family. They developed a deep love for German hymnody and always worked closely together. Their first book of translations, *Hymns from the Land of Luther,* was the beginning of a series of over one hundred hymns.

One cannot always tell who translated which hymn, but Jane is generally credited with putting into English "Be Still My Soul" (words by Catharina von Schlegel). It is thought that Catharina von Schlegel was the head of the Lutheran Home for Women connected with the ducal court in Cothen, Germany. Bach was organist in Cothen from 1717–1722, and because of the pietistic atmosphere of the Calvinistic reformed church, this is where Bach wrote much of his secular music.

Part of the popularity of "Be Still My Soul" is due to the beautiful melody from *Finlandia* by Sibelius.

> *Be still, my soul: the Lord is on thy side;*
> *Bear patiently the cross of grief or pain;*
> *Leave to thy God to order and provide;*
> *In ev'ry change He faithful will remain.*
> *Be still, my soul: thy best, thy heavenly Friend*
> *Through thorny ways leads to a joyful end.*
> *Be still, my soul: When dearest friends depart,*
> *And all is darkened in the vale of tears,*
> *Then shalt thou better know His love, His heart,*
> *Who comes to soothe thy sorrow and thy fears.*
> *Be still, my soul: Thy Jesus can repay*
> *From His own fullness all He takes away.*

10

Phillips Brooks
1835–1893

Character, and character only,
is the thing that is eternally powerful
in this world . . . character now,
and character forever!

PHILLIPS BROOKS

It was Christmas Eve 1865, and a young minister stood on the hill overlooking Bethlehem where the shepherds had watched their flocks on the night Jesus was born. The impression of that starry night never left Phillips Brooks. Three years later he was asked to write a hymn for the children of his Philadelphia parish for their Christmas service. The words of "O Little Town of Bethlehem" were already in his mind, the exquisite carol that has ministered the quiet beauty of God's Christmas gift to the human heart. Brooks's church organist, Lewis Redner, set the words to music, declaring that the tune was "a gift from heaven."

In 1891 Brooks became the Protestant Episcopal Bishop in Massachusetts. From this position he took a strong stand against the dangers of the Unitarian movement. He was an outstanding preacher and probably the most highly esteemed clergyman of his day. His deep earnestness and poetic insight, combined with a certain eloquence, made a strong impression on his listeners. But speaking and writing were always hard for him. He said once that speeches were like "towing ideas out to sea and then escaping by small boats in the fog."

Brooks was a handsome man, with a kind of nobility and purity of character, a giant in spirit and body—six feet, six inches tall. Though he never married, he loved children. His presence in a home was so exciting that it seemed to penetrate the whole house. Like a picture from *Alice in Wonderland*, he would romp on the floors with the little ones or stand as Goliath for some small grinning David with a sling. He always kept toys in his study for the many children who visited him.

At his funeral a speaker gave Brooks this tribute: "No more signal example has this generation seen of that deep work which the Holy Spirit accomplishes when He takes possession of the whole man." Phillips Brooks was a great man, with a great mind and a great heart.

> *O little town of Bethlehem,*
> *How still we see thee lie!*
> *Above thy deep and dreamless sleep*
> *The silent stars go by.*
> *Yet in thy dark streets shineth*
> *The everlasting light—*
> *The hopes and fears of all the years*
> *Are met in thee tonight.*

11

John Bunyan
1628–1688

As I walked through
the wilderness of this world.

JOHN BUNYAN

John Bunyan's life provides a prime example of evil turning into good. He wrote his masterpiece of religious allegory, *The Pilgrim's Progress*, from a prison cell. This exciting adventure story has been translated into more than one hundred languages and still delights old and young in all parts of the world.

Bunyan was born near Bedford, England, and as a boy received scant education. Like his father, he became a tinker, a maker and mender of utensils. At seventeen John served in the army of the Puritan Oliver Cromwell during the English civil war. Here he stored in his vivid imagination military scenes and adventures later used with such telling effect in his books.

At twenty he married his first wife, through whose influence he gradually abandoned his reckless way of living. His wife's sole dowry was two Christian books, *The Plain Man's Pathway to*

Heaven and *The Practice of Piety*. These books awakened Bunyan's interest in God. After long, intense, painful struggles he
was converted to Christ and became a nonconformist Baptist
minister. He spoke with such fervor and eloquence that people
flocked to hear him.

In 1661 Bunyan was arrested and thrown into prison for his
preaching. He spent twelve years in confinement, with brief
intervals of liberty. At any time he might have been set free by
promising to give up preaching, but he said, "If you let me out
today, I will preach again tomorrow." How painful it was to be
separated from his family, especially from his blind daughter
Mary, but God turned it to good.

While in prison he wrote not only *The Pilgrim's Progress*, a
world classic, but also *Grace Abounding to the Chief of Sinners* (his
spiritual autobiography), and *The Holy War*. Undoubtedly his
books would never have been written had he not been imprisoned.

Bunyan had a profound knowledge of the Bible. He absorbed
its words until they became his own. Luther's *Commentary on the
Epistle to the Galatians* and *Foxe's Book of Martyrs* also influenced
him. Though he knew no other literature, *Pilgrim's Progress* is an
amazing literary masterpiece.

Through his writings and preaching Bunyan related the
truth of the Scriptures to everyday life. For him the world was
exclusively the scene of spiritual warfare, and the most important
thing was the salvation of the soul. His style was simple and
imaginative, and he wrote in a language ordinary people could
understand. His writings had a great influence on English social
history.

Some years ago while visiting Bedford, England, where

Bunyan had been imprisoned, the authors asked a waitress in a local restaurant if she knew where Bunyan's museum was. She had never heard of him and called over the manager of the restaurant. He looked quite puzzled and suggested that we ask at the local library. Shrugging our shoulders as we left, we happened to glance across the street. There stood a large statue of the great Puritan, John Bunyan! How easily the important things in life can be missed.

The theme of *The Pilgrim's Progress* appears also in one of Bunyan's hymns, "He Who Would Valiant Be." Bunyan saw the Christian life as a pilgrimage, a constant moving along the way of holiness from this world of trials and tears to that beautiful one to come. He makes it clear that to be a pilgrim is no easy affair. It calls for great resources of faith, courage, endurance, and good cheer.

> *He who would valiant be*
> *'Gainst all disaster,*
> *Let him in constancy*
> *Follow the Master.*
> *There's no discouragement*
> *Shall make him once relent*
> *His first avow'd intent*
> *To be a pilgrim.**

---

*Adapted by Percy Dearmer. From *The English Hymnal,* 1906.

12

Elizabeth Clephane
1830–1869

Teach me, my God and King,
in all things Thee to see.
And what I do in anything,
to do it as for Thee.

GEORGE HERBERT

Elizabeth Clephane was born in Fife, Scotland. Perhaps because both her parents died early in life, she was a quiet, sensitive child. She led her classes at school, engrossed in the books and poetry which heightened her vivid imagination.

However, she did not lose touch with reality. The needs and sorrows of people around her became her concern as she grew to adulthood. She kept very little income for herself and gave most of what she had to others. The thankful people in her neighborhood called her "the sunbeam."

Elizabeth died at the age of thirty-nine. Four years later, one of her poems, "The Ninety and Nine," appeared in a Glasgow newspaper. According to E. E. Ryden in *The Story of Christian Hymnody*, it so happened that a songleader named Ira Sankey bought a copy of the newspaper just before getting on the train.

He found the poem and tried to read the words to D. L. Moody, his traveling companion. But the great evangelist was engrossed in his mail from the U.S.A. Sankey clipped the poem from the newspaper and slipped it into his pocket.

The two men were on an evangelistic tour in Scotland. At the meeting the following day in Edinburgh before a huge crowd, Moody spoke about the Good Shepherd. After he finished his message, he asked Horatius Bonar, the great Scottish preacher and hymn writer, if he would say a word to the audience. When Dr. Bonar concluded his remarks, Moody turned to Sankey and asked him if he had an appropriate hymn to sing. As Sankey explained it later, "I had nothing suitable in mind and was greatly troubled what to do . . . At this awful moment, I seemed to hear a voice say, 'Sing the hymn you found on the train!'"

Sankey reached in his pocket, withdrew the clipping, and placed it on the organ, praying the whole time that the Lord would help him sing the words so the people might hear and understand. As he said, "I struck the key of A-flat and began to sing." Note by note the melody came, and the music for "The Ninety and Nine" has not been changed from that day to this!

Later Ira Sankey received a letter from a woman who had attended the meeting in Edinburgh. She told him that the words had been written by her sister, Elizabeth Clephane, who had died five years before. The sister expressed delight that Elizabeth's poem had found a place in the service of Christ.

This hymn expresses the matchless love of the Good Shepherd for the sheep who wanders from the fold. It is based on the text, "Rejoice with me for I have found my sheep which was lost."

In the same year that she penned "The Ninety and Nine,"

Elizabeth Clephane wrote another favorite hymn, "Beneath the Cross of Jesus." It expresses the great, central fact of the Lamb of God as the ultimate and final authority in all of life and death: "Content to let the world go by, to know no gain nor loss; My sinful self my only shame, My glory all the cross."

Although the author did not live to hear the words of her poems set to music, millions of people have since heard her words and love to sing her hymns.

Some prominent businessmen who graduated from Yale about fifty years ago were asked to reflect on the question: If you had your life to live over again, what would you have preferred to accomplish? A president of a prestigious firm wistfully explained that he wished he had written a good song or a good book that people would continue to enjoy.

Elizabeth Clephane wrote two enduring hymns, never knowing they would be sung on into eternity. There is much evidence in the lives of hymn writers and poets that if you do one creative thing prayerfully and from the depth of your heart, it is possible many others will benefit.

Beneath the cross of Jesus
I fain would take my stand,
The shadow of a mighty Rock,
Within a weary land:
A home within the wilderness,
A rest upon the way,
From the burning of the noon-tide heat,
And the burden of the day.

13

William Cowper
1731–1800

*His simple poems of nature and
rural domestic life are a forerunner
of the works of the English romantic
poets of the early 1800s.*

HAROLD SCHWEIZER

First Corinthians 1:27 describes William Cowper exactly:
"God chose the weak things of the world to shame the
strong." A shy, fragile, gentle man, Cowper suffered all his life
from attacks of depression and despair which led to periods of
insanity and suicide attempts.

His mother died when he was only six years old. Soon after
this shock, he suffered a traumatic experience at a boarding school.
The older boys persecuted him unmercifully because of his shyness
and insecurity. Later, on the insistence of his father, he studied law.
But he did not like the legal profession and never practiced.

Once he was placed in a mental institution for eighteen
months. There a Christian doctor gave Cowper something better
than all the therapy he received. Cowper left the institution a
Christian. He then moved to Olney where John Newton could
be his minister and teach him more about the Christian faith.

It was Newton who urged him to write hymns, and through these hymns Cowper first became known to the world. Newton believed that writing hymns would help Cowper through his melancholy. The troubled man wrote many optimistic verses that did not reflect his inner feelings but did help to steer him away from insanity. The "Olney hymns" were published in 1779, including 68 written by Cowper and 286 by Newton. As with many great and meaningful hymns of the church, the writer's physical and mental suffering gave power and beauty to his poems. Among the finest of these Olney hymns are "Oh, for a Closer Walk with God!" "There Is a Fountain Filled with Blood," and "God Moves in a Mysterious Way."

One thought tormented Cowper all his life: "It is all over with you. You are perished." Often he managed to keep the dark moods at bay by gardening, visiting the sick, caring for his numerous pets, and studying nature. In Olney he lived in the home of a wonderful friend, Mrs. Mary Unwin, a bright, well-read woman with a strong faith. She and her children cared for him with special tenderness. He had gone to stay for two weeks; he remained for twenty-two years. Here his life passed quietly, and he assisted Newton as a lay curate.

Cowper would probably never have had a literary career had he not been urged to do so. Believing that writing would occupy his mind, Mrs. Unwin suggested that he write poetry. Always modest about his abilities, he followed her counsel like a child, and it did help him overcome some of his depression.

Some of Cowper's work, such as "The Diverting History of John Gilpin," shows a surprising humor, coming from such a sad life. He confessed that in writing his lighthearted poems he forced himself to be merry: "Despair made amusement necessary."

He did not write his best poems until he was nearly fifty years old. His major work was a 5,000-line poem called "The Task," in which he expresses love for the country and a distaste for city life. As he said, "God made the country, and man made the town." Today even Cowper's letters are considered a literary treasure.

When Mrs. Unwin died, Cowper once again became depressed. Only at intervals was he able to carry on his literary work. The bishop who visited him shortly before Cowper died said, "About half an hour before his death, his face, which had been wearing a sad and hopeless expression, suddenly lighted up with a look of wonder and inexpressible delight. It was as though he saw his Savior and as if he realized the blessed fact, 'I am not shut out of heaven after all!'"* Those who attended his funeral said this look of wonder remained even as he lay in his coffin.

> *Sometimes a light surprises*
> *The Christian while he sings;*
> *It is the Lord, who rises*
> *With healing in His wings:*
> *When comforts are declining,*
> *He grants the soul again*
> *A season of clear shining,*
> *To cheer it after rain.*

---

*From Ruben P. Halleck, *History of English Literature* (New York: American Book Company, 1900).

14

Fanny J. Crosby
1820–1915

That which moves the heart
most is the best poetry;
it comes nearest unto God,
the source of all power.

WALTER LANDOR

When Fanny Crosby was six weeks old, a slight cold caused an inflammation in her eyes. The family physician was called, but he was not at home. Someone else came in his place. The stranger recommended the use of hot poultices, which tragically resulted in the loss of her sight. As the sad event became known throughout her neighborhood, the man left town, and no one ever heard from him again. Concerning this tragedy, Miss Crosby wrote, "In more than eighty-five years, I have not for a moment felt a spark of resentment against him, for I have always believed from my youth up that the good Lord, in His infinite mercy, by this means consecrated me to the work that I am still permitted to do."

Fanny Crosby was an overcomer. "One of the earliest resolves that I formed in my young heart," she said, "was to leave all care to yesterday and to believe that the morning would bring forth its own peculiar joy."

The chief influences in her younger days were her mother and grandmother. As much as they could, they educated her at home. Her father had died when she was one year old. When the grandmother heard that the little child was blind and nothing could be done about it, she said, "Then I will be her eyes."

And she was. She described to the blind child the wonderful variety of colors in nature, the beauty of a sunrise and sunset, what the birds and flowers looked like, the colors in the sky. In time Fanny was describing these wonders better than a person with sight.

Also, the grandmother patiently taught Fanny the Bible, first one verse, then two. Soon Fanny was memorizing entire chapters. Her mind developed into a wonderful memory bank. She learned to play the guitar, and when she started to write songs, she would accompany herself.

When Fanny Crosby was fifteen, she entered the School for the Blind in New York City, although it was dreadfully hard for her to leave the safety of home. She was a student at the institution for seven years and then taught there for eleven years. Many important people visited the school in these years, and it became a custom to have Fanny recite her poems for them.

In 1843 Fanny Crosby went to Washington, DC, with other blind friends to prove to government leaders that blind people can be educated if they have the proper training. The first woman ever to speak before the Senate, she moved many senators to tears with her poems and winning personality. She became a friend of several presidents.

When she was in her thirties, Fanny Crosby married Alexander Van Alstyne, a scholarly, accomplished musician, also blind. He took great pride in his wife's genius and insisted that she retain her maiden name. They had one child, who died in infancy.

In 1850 when she heard a revival choir sing, "Here, Lord, I give myself away; 'tis all that I can do," she dedicated herself and her talents to God in a fresh way.

Fanny Crosby was always writing poems, but her hymn writing period did not begin until she was in her forties. One day she met the composer W. B. Bradbury, who requested that she write some hymns.

In 1864 she submitted her first hymn. Right away Bradbury was pleased with her words and told her, "As long as I have a publishing house, you will always have work." And so in a period of nine years, Fanny Crosby wrote "Safe in the Arms of Jesus," "Blessed Assurance," "Pass Me Not, O Gentle Savior," "Jesus, Keep Me Near the Cross," "I Am Thine, O Lord," "All the Way My Savior Leads Me," "Praise Him, Praise Him," "To God Be the Glory," "Rescue the Perishing," "A Wonderful Savior Is Jesus My Lord," "Jesus Is Tenderly Calling Thee Home," and many others! She was the leading poet of the "gospel hymn movement" associated with D. L. Moody and Ira Sankey.

Fanny Crosby was one of the most prolific poets in history. Often critics claim that her hymns do not possess a high poetic quality. She would be the first to agree with them. She was not writing for literary critics. She wanted her words to be understood by common people. She had lived among the poor most of her life, and she was directing her message particularly to them.

Yet her hymns have the universality to be sung by kings and queens, presidents and intellectuals as well.

Most of her hymns she wrote after midnight, as she needed silence to concentrate. She never was much of a sleeper. However, some of her hymns were written spontaneously. For example, a friend, Mrs. Joseph F. Knapp, asked Fanny to write words to some music she had composed. Mrs. Knapp played the melody over two or three times on the piano, and then asked Fanny if the music said anything to her. Immediately, Fanny replied, "Blessed assurance, Jesus is mine." Shortly after that, Fanny handed to the astonished friend the completed lyrics!

"Safe in the Arms of Jesus" came almost as fast. One day Dr. Doane, a manufacturing company president and an outstanding writer of hymn tunes, came into the office where Fanny Crosby was talking with Mr. Bradbury.

"Fanny," said William Doane, "I have just written a tune, and I want you to write a hymn for it."

She listened to the melody, retired to an adjoining room, and within half an hour returned with the lyrics. Dr. Doane wrote music for some of Fanny's most beloved hymns.

At the age of sixty, Fanny Crosby was more active than many people in their forties. Besides her hymn writing, she began a second career as a home mission worker. She now spent several days a week in the missions of the Bowery district in New York City, one of America's most depressing places. It was here she wrote "Rescue the Perishing."

She always insisted, "You can't save a man by telling him of his sins. He knows them already. Tell him there is pardon and love waiting for him . . . make him understand you believe in him, and never give up." Fanny Crosby did not simply say words; she lived her poems. That she knew how to listen and talk to people with desperate needs is evident from this story told by Bernard Ruffin in his book *Fanny Crosby*.

One time a man came in to a service and sat down in front of her. First she prayed quietly, and then she began to speak to him.

"Are you fond of music?" she asked.

"Yes."

"Wouldn't you like to stay for our evening service?"

"No."

"Well," said Fanny cheerfully, "will you allow me to come and sit down by you and talk to you?"

"Yes, I would like to have you."

She spoke for a long time to the rough, bedraggled man on subjects that interested him. Finally she said, "Do you know what the three sweetest words are in any language?"

"No, will you tell me?"

Fanny replied, *"Mother, home, and heaven."*

The man was quiet for a long time, lost in thought. Finally, he said softly, "My mother was a Christian."

He stayed for the service, and at the close of the meeting went to the altar, but not until Fanny promised to go with him.

Hundreds of stories can be told of how she helped so many of these people with their sad, broken lives. Hymns such as "Rescue the Perishing" and "Saved by Grace" penetrate the hearts of those who are perishing and need to be saved.

Fanny Crosby was an excellent speaker, and in her nineties she was still addressing large crowds. A local newspaper reported that she was "feeble in body, yet strong in mind . . . with a trust and faith in God as firm as the everlasting hills." Though bent nearly double by now and extremely thin, she wrote happily to a friend, "I am so busy I hardly know my name." And as she grew older, her cheerfulness increased rather than diminished.

In one of her last messages she said, "God will answer your prayers better than you think. Of course, one will not always get exactly what he has asked for. . . . We all have sorrows and disappointments, but one must never forget that, if commended to God, they will issue in good. . . . His own solution is far better than any we could conceive."

A Scottish minister told her it was too bad God did not give her the gift of sight. She startled him by responding, "If I had been given a choice at birth, I would have asked to be blind . . . for when I get to Heaven, the first face I will see will be the One who died for me."

> *Praise Him! praise Him! Jesus, our blessed Redeemer;*
> *Sing, O earth! His wonderful love proclaim!*
> *Hail Him! Hail Him! highest archangels in glory;*
> *Strength and honor give to His holy name.*
> *Like a shepherd, Jesus will guard His children,*
> *In His arms He carries them all day long.*
> *Praise Him! praise Him! tell of His excellent greatness;*
> *Praise Him! praise Him! ever in joyful song.*

Some of the material in this chapter was reprinted with permission from *Fanny Crosby* by Bernard Ruffin. A Pilgrim Press book from United Church Press © 1976, New York, NY.

15

Philip Doddridge
1702–1751

*O happy day that fixed my choice
On Thee, my Savior and my God!*

<small>PHILIP DODDRIDGE</small>

The son of a London oil merchant, Philip Doddridge was the last born of twenty children. He was so small at birth that the nurse, thinking he could not live, wrapped him in cotton and laid him in a little box. Fortunately, he was rescued.

When he was a little older, his mother taught him the Scriptures. His parents, devout Christians, died when Philip was still quite young, but loving neighbors took him into their home. Later he found another friend in Rev. Samuel Clarke, a Presbyterian minister who supported him in his studies.

Eventually Doddridge became a fine pastor and the head of an academy to which young men from all parts of the British Isles came to study. A brilliant scholar, he did the work of practically a whole faculty—teaching Hebrew, Greek, algebra, trigonometry, logic, philosophy, and divinity. Due in no small measure to his influence, the Congregationalists avoided following several Presbyterian groups into Unitarianism. Doddridge distributed Bibles both at home and abroad, helping pioneer nonconformist mission work. In addition, out of his deep compassion for the poor came a school and an infirmary dedicated to their relief.

As a hymn writer Doddridge ranks among the foremost in England. With their personal warmth, tenderness, and celebration of God's grace, his hymns resemble those of Watts, though they lack the strength and majesty. Doddridge composed hymns for his congregation to illustrate his sermons and gave them out line by line from the pulpit.

In 1730 he married Mercy Maris, a woman of intelligence and good judgment. They were a devoted couple.

Doddridge's accomplishments are amazing, considering that he struggled with poor health for years. In 1751 he and his wife journeyed to Lisbon, hoping that warmer air would help. The new scenery and gentle air raised his spirits briefly, and he said to his wife, "I cannot express what a morning I have had. Such delightful views of the heavenly world is my Father now indulging me with, as no words can express." Soon afterward he died and was buried there. His life is an inspiration, especially to those with fragile health, to persevere with the strength of the Lord.

> *Awake, my soul, stretch every nerve,*
> *And press with vigor on!*
> *A heavenly race demands thy zeal,*
> *And an immortal crown,*
> *And an immortal crown.*

16

Timothy Dwight
1752–1817

*His is the most important name in
early American hymnology.*

E. E. RYDEN

Timothy Dwight was the grandson of Jonathan Edwards, the
famous minister of Puritan New England whose powerful
sermons led to the Great Awakening in the 1730s and 1740s. In
his early years Dwight was educated by his mother, and before he
was four years old was able to read the Bible. After graduating
from Yale with highest honors at seventeen, he served as a chaplain with George Washington during the Revolutionary War.
Throughout the conflict he wrote songs to encourage the
American troops. Later as a pastor, he became noted for his
preaching throughout New England.

From 1795 until his death Dwight was president of Yale.
When he assumed office, he found a student body infected with
the "free thought" of Thomas Paine, Rousseau, and the French
Revolution. Many denied the deity of Christ, the inspiration of

the Bible, and the existence of miracle. In 1800 only one grad-uate was a church member. Dwight's dynamic preaching against the naturalism of the day ignited a spiritual revival on campus which soon spread to other New England schools. Yale became a center from which many clergymen carried evangelical truths to other places in the United States and around the world.

Not only did Dwight transform the spiritual climate of the school, but he raised academic standards and tripled the enroll-ment. He was a great leader and a remarkable teacher, exerting a decisive influence that lasted for many years.

All during this time, Dwight had continued to pursue his writing. He and a group of writers, most associated with Yale College, formed a literary center. Dwight wrote numerous poems, including the first American epic, titled "The Conquest of Canaan." His poetry was ranked by the reading public of that day as genius.

For the last forty years of his life, Dwight was unable to read consecutively for more than fifteen minutes at a time. A case of smallpox had left him with agonizing pain in his eyes. Yet noth-ing hindered his steadfast work for the Lord!

Dwight's hymn "I Love Thy Kingdom, Lord" (1800) may be the earliest hymn of American origin still in common use today. Many of his other hymns were paraphrases of the Psalms.

I love Thy kingdom, Lord,
The house of Thine abode—
The Church our blest Redeemer saved
With His own precious blood.

17

Charlotte Elliott
1789–1871

*There is no such raw material for
songs that live from heart to heart
as that furnished by sorrow.*

F. B. Meyer

Charlotte Elliott was born near Brighton, England, and grew up in a cultured and spiritual atmosphere. Her grandfather was the celebrated Evangelical preacher Henry Venn, and her father and brother were also ministers.

When Charlotte was in her early thirties, she suffered a serious illness that left her in poor health for the rest of her life. She often endured severe physical distress and, equally hard, the resulting sense of weakness, depression, and uselessness.

One day when her pain made her unusually irritable, the family had a visitor, Dr. Caesar Malan, a Swiss minister and musician. He noticed that Charlotte seemed restless and unhappy. He felt certain that she did not have peace in her heart, and he decided to ask her directly if she was a Christian.

She deeply resented his frank question and told him that she did not wish to discuss religion. He replied gently that he would not pursue a subject that displeased her, but that he spoke about it only because he wished she could experience God's peace in her life.

As time went by, Charlotte could not dismiss his words from her troubled mind. According to Christopher Knapp (*Who Wrote Our Hymns?*), one day when she was feeling better, she took courage and went to Dr. Malan to apologize for her rudeness. She admitted that she really did want to be a Christian. Yet thinking of her few good works, the depth of her pride and alienation from God, she said she would first have to make herself more worthy to come to Christ.

"I want to be saved; I want to come to Jesus," she said with a deep sigh, "but I don't know how."

Dr. Malan looked directly at Charlotte and replied, "Come to Him just as you are."

These simple, true words were sufficient. Charlotte Elliott came to the Savior just as she was, and immediately peace filled her heart. But, of course, there are always days when God's peace seems far away because our burdens are heavy. About fourteen years after her conversion, Charlotte was spending some time in the home of her brother, H. V. Elliott. There was activity and excitement in the parsonage as the family and friends were preparing a special bazaar to raise money to found a school for underprivileged children.

The day of the bazaar came, and everyone left in high spirits to go to the church. Charlotte was too weak to go with them, and as she slumped back on the couch, again she had the helpless feeling that she was doing nothing to serve her Lord. Deeply depressed, she reflected on her apparent uselessness.

While in this intense struggle and in a moment of great bodily pain, she reached for her pen and paper. The words she wrote were a comfort to her and lifted her burdened heart:

> *Just as I am, without one plea,*
> *But that Thy blood was shed for me,*
> *And that Thou bidd'st me come to Thee,*
> *O Lamb of God, I come, I come.*

The hymn first appeared anonymously in a paper edited by Miss Elliott. A wealthy woman was deeply moved by the words and had them printed in leaflet form to be distributed freely in England. One day Charlotte's doctor, after giving her a routine checkup, handed her a printed sheet, saying that he thought she would appreciate the sentiment of the words on it. The surprise and joy were mutual when she recognized her own hymn, and the doctor discovered that his patient was the author!

Though weak in body most of her life, Charlotte Elliott possessed a strong imagination and intellect. In spite of much suffering, her hymns show gentleness, patience, and spiritual strength. Often she could not attend church because of her frailty. She told her sister that her Bible was her church, always open, and there her High Priest ever waited to receive her. There she had her confessional, her thanksgiving, her psalms of praise, a field of promises—all she could want.

Years later when the hymn had become well-known in England, Charlotte's brother wrote that in the course of a long ministry, he had seen some fruit, but he felt far more had been done by this single hymn of hers.

D. L. Moody said this hymn of Charlotte Elliott drew as many people to the Lord in his fruitful evangelistic meetings as the words he spoke.

As a young man, Billy Graham was converted during a church service, and he walked to the altar while "Just As I Am" was being sung. Since then he has spoken to more people about Christ than any other person in history. In his crusades on every continent, he uses the hymn that meant so much to him.

God used an invalid to bless the world through words of comfort and consolation. After Charlotte's death, more than a thousand letters were found among her papers expressing gratitude for the help of this hymn. "Just As I Am" has been called the world's greatest soul-winning hymn. It is sung most often to the tune composed by Dr. William Bradbury, a leading composer of "Sunday school" songs.

> *Just as I am, Thy love unknown*
> *Has broken ev'ry barrier down;*
> *Now to be Thine, yea, Thine alone,*
> *O Lamb of God, I come.*

18

John Fawcett
1740–1817

We share our mutual woes,
Our mutual burdens bear:
And often for each other flows
The sympathizing tear.

JOHN FAWCETT

At age sixteen John Fawcett was converted under the fiery preaching of George Whitefield. Later, while serving as the minister of a small Baptist congregation in a Yorkshire village, he received a call to a prominent London church. He was pleased at the prospect of a larger salary and a larger group of people to lead in God's ways.

The day came when Fawcett preached his farewell sermon and, with the help of friends, loaded his household goods into a number of wagons. At the tears and farewells of the congregation his wife exclaimed, "Oh, John, I cannot bear this! I know not how to go!"

"Nor do I," he replied. Then he said with determination, "Get the men to unload the wagons and put everything in place as it was before."

This unusual experience* inspired John Fawcett to write the familiar hymn, "Blest Be the Tie That Binds." He sacrificed ambition and personal interest to remain with the people who loved him so deeply. For more than fifty years, he labored in the Yorkshire village at a modest salary. During these years he opened a school for young preachers. For his faithful and diligent service in this village, he received a doctor of divinity degree from Brown University.

His life demonstrates that we do not need to advance to higher positions, but we should be content with what the Lord would have us do. Had the Fawcetts gone to London, we probably would never have the joy and comfort of singing:

> *Blest be the tie that binds*
> *Our hearts in Christian love!*
> *The fellowship of kindred minds*
> *Is like to that above.*

---

*From Kenneth Osbeck, *101 Hymn Stories* (Grand Rapids: Kregel Publications, 1982).

19

A. Catherine Hankey
1834–1911

*'Tis a question whether
adversity or prosperity
makes the most poets.*

GEORGE FARQUHAR

K ate Hankey grew up in the suburb of Clapham near London. Her father was a prosperous banker and member of an Evangelical group working to abolish slavery and the slave trade in the British Empire. This group, led by William Wilberforce, wanted to apply Christian ethics to personal, social, political, national, and international affairs. As a result of their efforts, slavery was done away with in 1807.

Miss Hankey, like her father, had a caring attitude about people. She devoted much time to teaching the Bible to the affluent young ladies in her neighborhood. When she was only eighteen, she started a Bible class for girls working in the crowded factories and big shops in London. Her influence over this group was remarkable, and she had a close, warm relationship with the "factory girls" (as they were known in the wealthy Clapham enclave). These young women became very fond of

Kate, and some of them kept in touch with her all her life. Fifty years after the class no longer existed, five of these friends came to her funeral. Several members of her Bible class went on to become strong Christian leaders.

When Catherine Hankey was in her early thirties, she became very ill. Her recovery was long and painful. As she lay upon her bed, one recurrent thought went through her mind, *I wish someone would come and repeat the old, old story to me.*

(Those who have had long periods of convalescence know how encouraging it is when a Christian friend visits and helps refresh their faith. I remember a time when Jane was in St. Mary's Hospital in Rochester, Minnesota, recovering from a hip operation. Nigel Goodwin, head of "Genesis Arts" in England, came for a visit. The moment he entered the room, the two started talking excitedly about the arts in relation to Scripture. This visit was far better than a pain pill.)

Out of her long period of reflecting on the life and work of the Lord, Catherine Hankey wrote a fifty-verse poem on Christ and His love. From part one came the hymn "Tell Me the Old, Old Story," and "I Love to Tell the Story" is from part two.

The great songleader Ira Sankey, was one of those instrumental in increasing the popularity of "Tell Me the Old, Old Story," but Dr. William H. Doane wrote the music for this beloved hymn. He attended an international convention of the YMCA in 1867 where Major General Russell was to speak. Instead of giving the strong, powerful message the audience was expecting, the military leader said that he simply wanted to read a beautiful poem that should be the theme of everything they did there. He read "Tell Me the Old, Old Story."

Dr. Doane was so impressed with the words that he composed the music as he was traveling to his hotel. That evening several of the members of the YMCA gathered together and sang the hymn. Everyone admired the hymn, but no one realized how popular it would become.

As a result of a trip to South Africa to bring home an invalid brother, Catherine became interested in foreign missions. From then on, she devoted her income from writing to missions.

Always interested in bringing comfort to others, she spent the last year or so of her life visiting hospitals in London telling weary, lonely patients about God's love for them.

Nothing has more power to thrill us with sacred and tender memories than the hymns of the church, as we think about what we are singing and reflect upon the lives of those who have given us the words and music.

I love to tell the story,
Of unseen things above,
Of Jesus and His glory,
Of Jesus and His love.
I love to tell the story,
Because I know 'tis true;
It satisfies my longings,
As nothing else can do.
I love to tell the story,
'Twill be my theme in glory,
To tell the old, old story
Of Jesus and his love.

20

Frances Ridley Havergal
1836–1879

*She lived in the spirit of her
hymns and touched the world
with her words.*

E. E. RYDEN

M iss Havergal tells in her journal of a time when a workman
was painting outside her study. She opened the window to
ask how he was getting on. He told her that for months he had
been longing to speak to her about his desire to be "out and out
on the Lord's side."

She suggested that he climb off his perch on the high ladder
and step inside. Then followed a good talk, reading certain passages from the Bible, and prayer together. As a result, the painter
left her study happy that Jesus was henceforth his King as well as
his Savior.

Frances Ridley Havergal, one of the significant figures of the
Victorian Age, was born in Astley, Worcestershire, England. Her
middle name came from Nicholas Ridley, the great bishop who

was martyred at Oxford in 1555. Her mother and father were earnest Christians, and Frances was their youngest daughter.

Fanny, as she was called at home, was a bright, happy, vivacious child with a hungry mind. At the age of three, she could read well and was often found hiding under a table engrossed in a story. Her father, a minister of the Church of England and also a hymn writer, called Frances "Little Quicksilver."

Even though she had frail health and was never allowed to study regularly, by seven she was writing poems. Before long she was quoting the New Testament, Psalms, Isaiah, and the minor prophets. She learned Hebrew and Greek and also spoke several modern languages. Frances was an excellent pianist and loved singing.

When she was eleven, she learned that her mother was not going to live long. She refused to believe it. One of the last things the beloved mother told her sensitive child was, "Fanny dear, pray God to prepare *you* for all He is preparing *for* you." This became her lifelong prayer. At an early age she developed an unusually disciplined prayer life.

Sometime after the death of her mother, her father remarried. The stepmother came between father and daughter. This was a source of deep hurt to Frances, who had had such a close relationship with her mother and father. Though writing was difficult for her in this unsettled family situation, she persevered because of her discipline and faith. She knew her gifts were from God and wanted her writing and singing to be used to win people to the Lord. Early in her life she wrote, "I committed my soul to the Savior, and earth and heaven seemed brighter from that moment."

When she was eighteen, she developed an illness which

lasted for nine years. In this period she did little writing, but continued studying the Scriptures and praying.

Janet Grierson in her book, *Frances Ridley Havergal*, quotes Frances describing how she did her creative work: "Writing poetry is easy for me. Most of the time I just put down in verse a personal experience. Writing hymns is like praying, for I never seem to write even a verse by myself." She added with a smile, "I feel like a child writing. You know a child will look up at every sentence and ask, 'What shall I say next?' That is what I do. Every line and word and rhyme comes from God."

Her hymn "Like a River Glorious" (Isaiah 48:18) was composed in one of her periods of illness. Had she not had the courage to get up and move despite considerable pain and discomfort, this affliction could have left her an invalid. In most of her poems she urges believers in Christ not to complain in trial or sorrow.

Even though she never met Fanny Crosby, she admired Fanny's courage and her joy in the Lord. There was no doubt that Fanny Crosby thought highly of Frances, and they encouraged and enjoyed each other through letters and sharing poems.

In her twenties, Frances studied in Dusseldorf, Germany. It was here that she saw a painting of the Crucifixion with this engraving underneath it: "This I have done for thee; what hast thou done for Me?" In the previous century when the wealthy, young Count Zinzendorf read these same words, he had resolved to devote his life to serving God. Frances Ridley Havergal was also deeply moved. While standing in front of the painting, she reached into her bag for a piece of paper and a pencil and began writing the hymn, "Thy Life Was Given for Me."

Later after she had time to reread the poem, she thought it fell short of what she wanted to say and threw it into a stove. The crumpled paper fell out untouched by the flames. Some months later she showed the hymn to her father. He was moved to compose a melody for it, and this hymn which was nearly destroyed is still a blessing and a challenge to many.

Despite her poor health, Frances made several trips to Switzerland where she loved to climb mountains and take extended walks through the green valleys. Each time she was refreshed and inspired in the writing of her hymns.

On her last journey there, she spent time in Champery, the same small village where the Schaeffers began the work of L'Abri Fellowship. In Miss Havergal's study in England, one of the favorite pictures on the wall was *The Snow Peaks of the Dents du Midi*. At the present location of L'Abri in Huemoz, there is a sweeping view of Les Dents du Midi. Those of us who live here never tire of lifting our eyes to the mountains.

Frances Havergal's hymn "Take My Life, and Let It Be" was written in 1874, four years before she died. She was visiting in the home of a friend where there were several guests. Some of them had no knowledge of what it meant to be a Christian, and a number of others were half-hearted believers with no apparent joy in their lives. Suddenly Frances had a deep longing to be used by God to bring these people to a living faith in Christ.

After much earnest conversation, questions and answers, her prayer was answered. There was a time of rejoicing as the Holy Spirit revealed to these new friends what a comfort and joy it is to have the Lord Jesus Christ as Savior and King. She told her sister later that she was too happy to sleep that night, so she spent the time praying and writing, "Take my life, and let it be consecrated, Lord, to Thee. . . ."

In her last few years, Frances considered this hymn a measure of her own commitment to God. She constantly reviewed the words to renew her spiritual life. Those who knew her described her as one whose life was consecrated to loving and joyful service.

The second verse of the hymn has this thought: "Take my silver and my gold; not a mite would I withhold." These were not empty words for Frances. One time when she heard there was a need in India to teach the women the Bible, she packed up her jewels, nearly fifty pieces, saving only a few special gifts from family and friends, and sent them to the Church Missionary Society. She said she had never packed a box with such pleasure.

Frances Ridley Havergal was only forty-two when she died. When her physician told her that her condition was serious and that she did not have long to live, she told him that it was too good to be true. In her last moments she began singing "Golden Harps Are Sounding," for which she had written both the words and music. Her sister Maria said that there was a radiance on her face as she passed away—as though she had already seen her Lord.

Other fine hymns by Frances Ridley Havergal are "Lord, Speak to Me That I May Speak," "O Savior, Precious Savior," "I Am Trusting Thee, Lord Jesus," "Who Is on the Lord's Side?," "Thou Art Coming, O My Savior," and many more.

Carved on her tombstone by her own request are the words:

"The blood of Jesus Christ his Son cleanseth us from all sin"
—1 John 1:7

Oh fill me with Thy fulness, Lord,
Until my very heart o'erflow
In kindling thought and glowing word,
Thy love to tell, Thy praise to show.

21

Annie S. Hawks
1835–1918

For myself the hymn
["I Need Thee Every Hour"]
at its writing was prophetic
rather than expressive of
my own experiences.

ANNIE S. HAWKS

Annie S. Hawks, who is known best for her hymn "I Need Thee Every Hour," was born in Hoosick, New York. At the age of fourteen, she was already writing poems for a newspaper. When she married at twenty-four, she and her husband moved to Brooklyn. They became members of a church whose minister was a hymn writer and theologian, Dr. Robert Lowry.

When Dr. Lowry discovered that Mrs. Hawks had talent for writing, he encouraged her to use her gift to write hymns for which he might compose the music.

One day in 1872, Annie Hawks handed her pastor the poem, "I Need Thee Every Hour." Even though she wrote many other hymns, it is this one that has become a universal favorite and has been translated into many languages. Based on John

15:4, 5, the hymn is as meaningful to people today as it was more than a hundred years ago.

E. E. Ryden in *The Story of Christian Hymnody* relates that shortly before her death at the age of eighty-three, Annie Hawks was asked how she happened to write this hymn, which already was being sung in many countries. "I remember well the morning many years ago," replied Mrs. Hawks, "when in the midst of the daily cares of my home, I was so filled with a sense of the nearness to my Master that, wondering how one could live without Him either in joy or pain, these words, 'I need Thee every hour,' flashed into my mind. Seating myself by the open window in the balmy air of the bright June day, I caught up my pencil and the words were soon committed to paper, almost as they are being sung now."

She explained that she had written "I Need Thee Every Hour" at a time when her life was going smoothly and joyfully. It was not until years later when the stress of a great personal sorrow came upon her, undoubtedly the death of her husband, that she understood something of the comforting power in the words she had been permitted to give out to others.

One hears it over and over from these writers who have enriched us with their hymns that the words they put down, often in a brief period of time, were a gift from God.

"I Need Thee Every Hour" was discovered by Dwight L. Moody and Ira Sankey and was another hymn that brought many people to the Lord. Moody himself was not musical, but he had a keen appreciation of the possibilities of music in connection with his ministry. He made the singing of hymns a major feature of his meetings.

Of course, the Bible is the inspired Word of God and all we

need for salvation, as well as for direction in our daily living. Yet it is wonderful that the Holy Spirit continues to inspire the great hymns of the church, and how needed they are. More than once when I have heard a moving sermon, the tears do not come to my eyes until we sing a favorite hymn at the end of the service. As Dr. Ryden said, "It is hardly a coincidence that every great spiritual movement in the history of the church has been accompanied by a fresh outburst of song."

> *I need Thee ev'ry hour, Most gracious Lord;*
> *No tender voice like Thine can peace afford.*
> *I need Thee, Oh, I need Thee,*
> *Ev'ry hour I need Thee;*
> *Oh, bless me now, my Savior,*
> *I come to Thee!*

22

Reginald Heber
1783–1826

Day and night they never stop saying:
"Holy, holy, holy is the Lord God Almighty,
who was, and is, and is to come."

REVELATION 4:8B

From childhood Reginald Heber loved books and could read the Bible with ease before he was five. "Reginald doesn't read books," his brother once said. "He devours them." One of Reginald's favorite books, *The Life of Henry Martyn*, kindled in him a profound missionary interest, especially for India. The book told of Martyn's travels through the Indian Empire (almost unknown at that time), of his heroic life, and of his martyrdom.

Even in his youth Reginald had a deep faith in the Lord. He was traveling once with his parents in the wild, hilly country of Yorkshire when they ran into a violent storm. His mother became frightened, and it was Reginald who reassured her, "Do not be afraid, Mama; God will look after us."

Heber's scholarly, well-to-do family sent him to Oxford where he became known for his brilliant gifts. Here he formed a special friendship with Sir Walter Scott. Eventually Heber was ordained in the Church of England and inherited the estate and the living from his father to become the country squire and clergyman of Hodent in Shropshire. He was deeply appreciated and loved by the congregation because of his compassion and winsome personality.

Heber understood the value and power of congregational singing and wrote his hymns with that in mind. One Saturday evening his father-in-law asked him to write a hymn with a strong message for the Sunday morning service. In twenty minutes Heber came up with "From Greenland's Icy Mountains"— the great missionary hymn.

Some of his other hymns are still loved today—"Brightest and Best of the Sons of the Morning," "The Son of God Goes Forth to War," and "Holy, Holy, Holy." Lord Tennyson, who admired the purity of language and sense of adoration in "Holy, Holy, Holy," described it as the world's greatest hymn.

In 1822 Reginald Heber became the preacher at Lincoln's Inn and that same year was offered the position of Bishop of Calcutta. After a great deal of hesitation, he finally went to India at the age of forty. The Diocese of India included Ceylon and all of Australia. It was not long before the arduous duties, including extensive travel, and the extremely hot weather affected his health. After three years he died, leaving his wife, Amelia, and two children. Heber is remembered most for his hymns, which were published after his death.

Shall we, whose souls are lighted,
With wisdom from on high,

Shall we to men benighted
The lamp of life deny?
Salvation! O salvation!
The joyful sound proclaim,
Till earth's remotest nation
Has learned Messiah's name.

23

George Herbert
1593–1633

*Good words are worth much
and cost little.*

GEORGE HERBERT

In the tall but frail frame of George Herbert existed an iron resolve. Once he made the choice between the world and God, he never faltered but devoted all of his gifts, desires, and possessions to his Lord.

Herbert was born into an aristocratic Welsh family. His father died when he was three, and later his mother remarried. She insisted that all of her ten children have a good education and tended to each carefully. A remarkable woman, she was a friend of the great poet, John Donne.

At the age of fifteen, George entered Cambridge and was graduated from Trinity College three years later. He became Public Orator for the university and was often at the court of King James I. When the king died, Herbert abandoned the empty glitter of the court at his devout mother's urging. He was ordained an Anglican clergyman in 1630. He spent the rest of his short life as rector at Bemerton, near Salisbury, where he was greatly loved by his congregation.

Herbert's poetry came out of his own spiritual struggles and from the comfort he found in caring for his flock. He was so modest he did not want his poems to be printed. He was writing to the glory of God, not for other people. However, after his death the collected poems, titled *The Temple*, were published, and today are regarded as among the best religious verse of the English Renaissance. Noted for a gentle piety, the poems join words gracefully and lovingly into grand hymns of praise to God. The main themes are Christian love and the eternal beauty of holiness.

Herbert was happily married to Jane Danvers. She had eight sisters, and her father had wanted Herbert to marry any one of his daughters, but especially Jane. Her father often spoke to Jane about the young cleric in such an enthusiastic way that she fell in love with George even before meeting him.

He numbered among his friends Lord Bacon, Bishop Andrews, and John Donne. George Herbert was a younger contemporary of William Shakespeare.

Like Martin Luther, Herbert was a skilled musician and often accompanied his own singing on the viol or lute. One can imagine him singing his lovely hymns, "Teach Me, My God and King," "The God of Love My Shepherd Is," or "Let All the World in Every Corner Sing."

> *Teach me, my God and King,*
> *In all things Thee to see,*
> *And what I do in anything,*
> *To do it as for Thee.*

24

William W. How
1823–1897

Here I am! I stand at the door
and knock. If anyone hears my voice
and opens the door, I will come in and
eat with him, and he with me.

REVELATION 3:20

When Queen Victoria made William How bishop of Bedford, with East London as his diocese, he worked tirelessly to improve conditions in that poverty-stricken district. Unlike most bishops of the time, who lived in fine houses and traveled in private coaches, How lived among the poor and rode the bus. He was affectionately known as the "poor man's bishop" or the "people's bishop" throughout the city of London. He loved most working among children, and nothing pleased him more than to be called the "children's bishop." According to Elsie Houghton in *Christian Hymn Writers*, "He loved the simple things of life: simple trust, simple character, simple childhood." How was probably one of the most beloved bishops in the Church of England during the last century.

It was when he became rector at Whittington, a farming village near Wales, that he began writing hymns. He once described a good hymn as "something like a good prayer—simple, real, earnest, and reverent." How's son commented, "It is the fate of a hymn writer to be forgotten. The hymn remains; the name of the writer passes away." But Bishop How did not mind. His goal was not to be remembered, but to be useful.

Several widely known hymns of his are "O Word of God Incarnate," "For All the Saints," which was set to vivacious music by Vaughan Williams, and "O Jesus, Thou Art Standing." This last hymn was undoubtedly inspired by Holman Hunt's celebrated painting *The Light of the World* picturing Christ patiently standing and knocking at a closed door.

> *O Jesus, Thou art standing*
> *Outside the fast-closed door,*
> *In lowly patience waiting*
> *To pass the threshold o'er;*
> *Shame on us, Christian brothers,*
> *His name and sign who bear,*
> *O shame, thrice shame upon us,*
> *To keep Him standing there!*

25

Julia Ward Howe
1819–1910

*A poet must sing for
his own people.*

EDMUND STEDMAN

At the age of ninety-two, Julia Ward Howe received an honorary degree from Smith College. As she was wheeled onto the platform, she received a standing ovation. After the presentation, the organist struck a chord, and the standing audience began to sing "Mine eyes have seen the glory of the coming of the Lord."

In 1861, after the Civil War had begun, Dr. Samuel G. Howe, his wife, Julia Ward Howe, their pastor from Boston, and the governor of Massachusetts were witnessing a review of northern troops under General McClellan near Washington, D.C. There was a sudden movement of the enemy, and the Howe party hurried back to Washington passing troop after troop all singing "John Brown's body lies amouldering in the grave." They heard it over and over.

When they were out of danger, Dr. Clarke, the minister, turned to Mrs. Howe. "That's a stirring melody, Julia, but can't you write better words for it?"

Mrs. Howe went to bed that night and slept quite soundly. Suddenly she awoke early in the morning and found her mind twirling with words. She told herself to get up and write down the verses lest she fall asleep again and forget them.

In the dimness of the dawn, she found a pen and began to put down on a scrap of paper the verses to the immortal "Battle Hymn of the Republic."

When she returned to Boston, she decided to show her poem to the editor of the *Atlantic Monthly*. He accepted it, suggested the title, and paid her five dollars (some historians say four dollars!). Soon after it was published, it became one of the greatest songs to come out of the Civil War. It has continued to find its way into practically every hymnal published since.

Julia Ward Howe was born in 1819 into a prominent New York City family. Her mother was a poet of some ability. A combination of tutors and private schools provided her with an excellent education in literature and languages. By the age of seventeen, she was writing poetry for leading magazines.

In 1843 she married Dr. Samuel G. Howe, the director of the Massachusetts State School for the Blind. The Howes had six children. Both she and her husband were sympathetic toward the Abolitionist movement and became enthusiastic crusaders. Julia continued to write poems and plays and to help her husband edit *The Commonwealth*. She published her first book of poetry, *Passion Flowers*, anonymously.

Though she wrote extensively on literary and cultural topics as well as on women's rights, Mrs. Howe's one enduring success is the "Battle Hymn of the Republic." Because of this hymn she was the only woman to be elected to the American Academy of Arts and Letters. Noted in her day as a lecturer and social reformer, she was the first person to introduce the idea of Mother's Day.

After the Civil War, Mrs. Howe actively crusaded for the unpopular cause of woman suffrage, helping to found the American Woman Suffrage Association. Later she worked for prison reform and world peace and visited wounded servicemen in hospitals. These experiences caused her to think deeply about the agony, the suffering, the dreadful price of war.

Shortly after the "Battle Hymn of the Republic" appeared in the Atlantic Monthly, Chaplain McCabe, an army volunteer from Ohio, read the poem in the magazine. He was able to memorize it by singing it through a few times.

Later he was captured by the Confederates and put in prison in Richmond. News came to the prisoners that the Union troops had lost thousands of men in battle. It is hard enough to be in prison, but believing they were on the losing side, they felt all hope was gone.

Suddenly someone burst into the prison to announce that the report had been an error and that the Union soldiers had been victorious. Chaplain McCabe began to sing, "Mine eyes have seen the glory of the coming of the Lord." The other prisoners joined in on the chorus, "Glory, glory, hallelujah!"

When Chaplain McCabe was released from prison, he went to Washington to speak to a Christian group. There he told about all the prisoners singing the "Battle Hymn of the

Republic." The audience requested that he sing it for them. When he finished, President Lincoln, with tears streaming down his face, asked him to sing it again.

This hymn continued to be sung by Union soldiers—camped at night or on the move or marching to battle. It is a song of freedom containing the injunction to "crush the serpent, slavery."

Although many tunes were written for "The Battle Hymn of the Republic," the tune Mrs. Howe preferred was written by William Steffe of Richmond, Virginia.

A recent U.S. stamp with the picture of Julia Ward Howe has been issued. No question about it, she was one of the outstanding women of her time. Her hymn is still sung on holidays and at patriotic meetings.

Mine eyes have seen the glory
of the coming of the Lord;
He is trampling out the vintage
where the grapes of wrath are stored!
He hath loosed the fateful lightning
of his terrible swift sword;
His truth is marching on.
Glory, glory, hallelujah!
Glory, glory, hallelujah!
Glory, glory, hallelujah!
His truth is marching on.

26

Thomas Ken
1637–1711

*. . . he came as near to the ideal
Christian perfection as human
weakness permits.*

Thomas Macaulay

Probably no four lines of any hymn are so well known as these by Thomas Ken:

> *Praise God, from whom all blessings flow;*
> *Praise Him, all creatures here below;*
> *Praise Him above, ye heavenly host;*
> *Praise Father, Son, and Holy Ghost.*

Thomas Ken was one of the first English writers to produce hymns that were not versifications of Psalms. He was an accomplished musician and poet and enjoyed singing his hymns while accompanying himself on the lute.

Left an orphan in early childhood, Thomas was taken into the home of his sister Ann and grew up under the guardianship of Izaak Walton, author of *The Compleat Angler*. One of Ken's delights was fishing with Walton in a nearby stream.

After graduating from Oxford, Ken became a tutor and later a clergyman in small parishes, first in Essex and then on the Isle of Wight. On returning to Winchester, he published "A Manual of Prayers" for students at Winchester College to use. He wrote three hymns for this manual, each with the same last stanza—the four lines that have become known as the Doxology. Louis Bourgeois, who was mainly responsible for the *Genevan Psalter* with its many beautiful melodies, was commissioned by John Calvin to write the music for Ken's great hymn.

In 1679 Ken was sent to The Hague as chaplain to the king's sister, Mary of Orange. But because of his outspoken denunciation of the corrupt lives of those in authority there, he was compelled to leave the following year.

In 1683 when the court was to visit Winchester, he refused King Charles II permission for his house to be used by the notorious Nell Gwynne. The king respected his decision and even appointed Ken Bishop of Bath and Wells in 1684. Charles referred to Ken as "the good little man." When attending chapel, the king would say, "I must go in and hear Ken tell me all my faults." During his tenure as the dissipated king's chaplain, Ken never lost Charles's favor.

When James II came to power, Thomas Ken and six other bishops were thrown into the Tower of London for refusing to read the second Declaration of Indulgence. Shortly afterward they were triumphantly freed.

In 1691 Ken refused to take the oath of allegiance to William and Mary and as a result lost his position as bishop. In poverty he retired to the home of a devoted friend, Lord Weymouth, and lived there quietly to a serene old age.

Thomas Ken was one of the most fearless preachers of his time, a man of rare piety and sweetness of spirit, concerned to do right. He was a heroic figure during a turbulent time in English history.

His superb evening hymn "All Praise to Thee, My God, This Night" and beautiful morning hymn "Awake, My Soul, and with the Sun" are still sung the world over.

> *All praise to Thee, my God, this night*
> *For all the blessings of the light;*
> *Keep me, O keep me, King of kings,*
> *Beneath Thine own almighty wings.*

27

Mary A. Lathbury

1841–1913

Whatever you do,
work at it with all your heart,
as working for the Lord,
not for men.

COLOSSIANS 3:23

Before his midweek service, the great London preacher G. Campbell Morgan always read the words to the hymn, "Break Thou the Bread of Life." The third verse is an excellent prayer for understanding God's truth.

O send Thy Spirit, Lord,
Now unto me,
That He may touch my eyes,
And make me see:
Show me the truth concealed
Within Thy Word,
And in Thy Book revealed
I see the Lord.

Mary Lathbury wrote this hymn. Born in a parsonage in Manchester, New York, she showed artistic tendencies even as a child. She particularly enjoyed drawing pictures of children.

When she graduated from school, she shared an art studio with her sister in New York where she also taught art. Her illustrations in magazines and periodicals made her name widely known. She also wrote books of poetry and illustrated them with sketches.

She enjoyed what she was doing, but she yearned to serve the Lord in a more complete way. The opportunity came when Dr. John Vincent, a Methodist clergyman, asked her to assist him in the Chautauqua movement as his secretary. He first conceived of the school as a summer instruction session for Sunday school teachers. Its location was ideal—a beautiful wooded area in New York state by the blue waters of Lake Chautauqua.

The growth and expansion of the Chautauqua movement for over a century had a strong influence on adult education in many countries. The first assembly was held at Chautauqua in August 1814. It expanded to include a series of clubs for young people interested in music, reading, fine arts, physical education, and religion. It also began one of the oldest correspondence schools in the U.S.A.

Dr. Vincent appreciated Mary's artistic talent, competence, and helpfulness. Whenever he wished to have a hymn that would fit into a study session of the Bible or a vesper service, he would ask her to write one. Music played a large part in the meetings.

When seeking inspiration, it was her custom to find a quiet spot overlooking the lake. While praying one day for guidance as to what to write, she began thinking of Christ feeding the five thousand by the Sea of Galilee. From her reflection came the widely known hymn, "Break Thou the Bread of Life."

Another hymn she wrote by the shore of Lake Chautauqua was "Day Is Dying in the West." This beautiful evening hymn quickly became a favorite at the vesper services. It is still sung as Christians gather to praise God and to remember that the Lord is with us now and forever. Critic E. E. Ryden said that this hymn is "one of the finest and most distinctive hymns of modern times." Originally she wrote two stanzas, but at the strong insistence of friends, she added two more verses ten years later.

Mary Lathbury became known as the "poet of Chautauqua." Those who knew her best tell of her indescribable charm, her gentle, Christian character, and the influence for good she had on other people because of her dedication to the Lord. She consecrated her gifts "to Him who is the best Friend that woman ever knew."

She founded a club, the Look-Up Legion, which attracted thousands of boys and girls to Christianity. The foundation rules were: "Look up and not down; look forward and not back; look out and not in; and lend a hand, in Jesus' name."

Break thou the bread of life,
Dear Lord, to me,
As thou didst break the loaves
Beside the sea;
Beyond the sacred page
I seek thee, Lord;
My spirit pants for thee,
O Living Word.

28

Jemima Luke
1813–1906

That understanding is the
noblest which knows not the
most but the best things.

SIR THOMAS MORE

Jemima Luke was born in London in 1813. Her father was involved with a ministry of supplying "floating" chapels for seamen, and he was the founder of the British and Foreign Sailors' Society. Undoubtedly she caught her interest in missionary work from him.

Jemima had a gift for writing, and by the age of thirteen was anonymously sending poems to *The Juvenile Magazine*. Some years later she edited *The Missionary Repository*, the first missionary magazine ever published for children. Some of the contributors were Livingstone, Moffat, and James Montgomery.

As well as a writer and editor, Jemima was a teacher. Cecilia Rudin in her book, *Stories of Hymns We Love*, relates an incident that happened one day when Jemima visited another school to observe. She watched the teachers march around the room to a tune (actually a Greek air called "Salamis"). She was intrigued with the melody.

She thought, *What a lovely children's hymn it would make if only that tune had suitable words.* Jemima spent considerable time searching through books and hymnals for appropriate words, but found none.

In 1841 on a beautiful spring morning she was riding alone in a stagecoach returning from a missionary journey. She started to hum the Greek melody. Suddenly words began to shape in her mind. Finding a wrinkled envelope in her pocket, she wrote them down, "I think when I read that sweet story of old, when Jesus was here among men . . ."

She taught the words and melody to her pupils, and the following Sunday they sang the hymn in the Sunday school class where her father was superintendent.

"Where did that hymn come from?" asked her father, obviously very pleased.

"Jemima made it!" was the happy answer of the excited children as they clapped their hands together.

The following day, her father sent a copy of the hymn to the *Sunday School Teachers' Magazine;* they printed it. The hymn continues to gladden many hearts.

This hymn describes in a few words the Lord's earthly ministry, His resurrection, His preparation of a heavenly home for believers, and His desire that none should perish. As the Lord says in Matthew 19:14: "Let the little children come to me, and do not hinder them, for the kingdom of heaven belongs to such as these." There is no more effective way of teaching children

Christian truth than by singing hymns. Their part and our part is to believe the words of Christ.

At one time Jemima was accepted as a missionary to India, but poor health prevented her from going. She never lost her zeal for the cause of missions. Because she could not achieve this goal in her life, she helped people who had needs nearby.

Probably because of her desire to be a missionary, she added a last stanza to her hymn later. No doubt it was her prayer that these words would reach some she could not speak to personally:

> *But thousands and thousands who wander and fall,*
> *Never heard of that heavenly home;*
> *I wish they could know there is room for them all,*
> *And that Jesus has bid them to come.*

Jemima married the Reverend Samuel Luke in 1843. She wrote a couple of books, which were published, but primarily she is remembered for this one hymn.

After her husband died in 1868, she continued helping others. Although she was unable to fulfill her dream of going to India as a missionary, as Christ said of Mary in Mark 14:8—"She did what she could." One of her many projects was seeing that homes were built for ministers who were too poor to afford adequate housing.

In 1904 an international convention of the Christian Endeavor Society was held in Baltimore. In *The Story of Christian Hymnody*, E. E. Ryden records the message Jemima sent to the young people:

Dear children, you will be men and women soon, and it is for you and the children of England to carry the message of a Savior's love to every nation of this sin-stricken world.

The Lord make you ever faithful to Him and unspeakably happy in His service! I came to Him at ten years of age, and at ninety-one can testify to His care and faithfulness.

> I think, when I read that sweet story of old,
> When Jesus was here among men,
> How he called little children as lambs to his fold,
> I should like to have been with him then.
> I wish that his hands had been placed on my head,
> That his arms had been thrown around me,
> That I might have seen his kind look when he said,
> "Let the little ones come unto me."

29

Martin Luther
1483–1546

*I feel strongly that all the arts,
and particularly music,
should be used in the service of Him
who has created and given them.*

MARTIN LUTHER

A s a young student, Martin Luther sang in the streets of
Eisenach to pay his school fees. One day a cultured woman,
Ursula Cotta, and her husband heard him singing. Observing how
fragile and needy he was, they invited him to live with them. In
the rich atmosphere of their home, Luther acquired a new thirst
for knowledge and was encouraged to sing and play the lute. Later
under Luther's influence music became a vital force in the spread
of the Reformation.

While studying law at the University of Erfurt, Luther and
a friend went walking through a forest. Suddenly lightning struck
his friend dead. Frightened, Luther begged God to spare his life
and vowed to give himself wholly to the Lord. He soon entered
a monastery, much to his parents' dismay.

As a young man, Luther was already puzzling over questions

that eventually led to the Reformation. The crucial question for him was how an individual finds favor with God. The harder he tried to please a holy God, the more hopeless he became.

While studying the Psalms and Paul's letters in the Latin Bible, he saw that God's favor is a gift to be accepted, not a prize to be won. Luther suddenly understood the meaning of justification solely by faith in God's grace, the doctrine for which he became famous. This doctrine involved Luther in controversy for the rest of his life, yet he went on to become one of the most influential men in history. While Professor of Theology at Wittenberg, he posted his ninety-five theses on the church door on that momentous day in 1517, launching the Protestant Reformation.

In his times of stress Luther had his faithful wife, Catherine, to comfort and encourage him. He said, "There is no more lovely, friendly, and charming relationship, communion, or company than a good marriage." They had five children. Luther's cradle song "Away in a Manger" and his Christmas hymn "From Heaven Above to Earth I Come" were written for his young son Hans.

Church historian Philip Schaff, calling Luther "the Ambrose of German hymnody," adds, "To Luther belongs the extraordinary merit of having given to the German people in their own language the Bible (a masterpiece of translation), the catechism, and the hymnbook, so that God might speak directly to them in His Word and that they might directly answer Him in their songs."

Luther's first German hymnal (1524) included the powerful "A Mighty Fortress Is Our God" (a paraphrase of Psalm 46). The hymnal contained sixteen hymns, most of which were written by Luther himself. By the time of his death, nearly sixty collections of hymns by various authors had appeared. Thus through Luther's efforts, congregational singing regained its rightful place in Christian worship, and modern hymnody had begun.

Singing played a large part in spreading Luther's teaching. Samuel Taylor Coleridge regards Luther as doing "as much for the Reformation by his hymns as by his translation of the Bible." The popularity of the Lutheran hymns was indeed astonishing; people everywhere began to sing. Luther's hymns opened a whole new era of music. Most of the hymn writers included in this book were influenced by Luther's example.

> *A mighty fortress is our God,*
> *A bulwark never failing;*
> *Our helper He, amid the flood*
> *Of mortal ills prevailing.*
> *For still our ancient foe*
> *Doth seek to work us woe;*
> *His craft and pow'r are great,*
> *And, armed with cruel hate,*
> *On earth is not his equal.*

30

Henry F. Lyte
1793–1847

*He became a power for good
and a person much loved.*

<small>ANONYMOUS</small>

H enry Lyte's father died when he was quite young, and it was Henry's godly, talented mother who wielded the major influence on his life. Despite the handicap of poverty, he struggled through college and won several prizes for poetry. He had intended to become a physician, but one day he received a call from a friend that changed the direction of his life.

This neighboring minister knew he was dying and had a fearful sense of being unprepared. Together the two men searched the Scriptures, particularly Paul's letters. The dying man came to a true understanding of the pardon and peace Christ alone can give and soon went to meet his Lord with joy. This experience deeply affected Lyte, so much that he abandoned medicine and began to prepare instead for the ministry.

When he took up his parish duties, Lyte led a very busy life.

A distinguished scholar, he wrote constantly, educated his own children, and composed hymns. One of his most popular hymns is "Praise My Soul, the King of Heaven," a paraphrase of Psalm 103.

But illness came to him very early. As the English climate played havoc with his weak lungs, Lyte spent his winters on the continent, especially in Rome where he had various friends and the weather seemed to suit him. Always he returned to his home in the summertime. As autumn approached in 1847, he wrote, "I am meditating flight again to the South . . . the swallows are inviting me to accompany them; and yet alas, while I am talking of flying, I am just able to crawl."* As he was about to give his farewell sermon in Brixham, his friends, knowing how weak he was, urged him not to preach; but he insisted, "It is better to wear out than to rust out."**

Later in the afternoon, Lyte walked by the shore as the sun was shining in a glory of crimson and gold on a peaceful Sunday evening. Soon afterward he handed his daughter the words of the immortal hymn, "Abide with Me." Its theme is the evening of life.

The same week, accompanied by his wife and son, he left home for Europe knowing he would never return. For years he had been distressed at the thought of dying, but God, who had given him grace to live, gave him grace to die. His last words were, "Joy! Peace!" He is buried in Nice, France.

In his lifetime Henry Francis Lyte was little known beyond Lower Brixham, England, where he labored among fishermen and sailors as curate of All Souls Anglican Church. A man who labored in obscure places, practically unnoticed, is remembered the world over for this beautiful hymn.

Abide with me: fast falls the eventide;
The darkness deepens; Lord, with me abide!
When other helpers fail, and comforts flee,
Help of the helpless, O abide with me.

---

*From Elsie Houghton, *Christian Hymn Writers* (Worcestor: Evangelical Press of Wales, 1982).

**From E. E. Ryden, *The Story of Christian Hymnody* (Rock Island, IL: Augustana Press, 1959).

31

John Milton
1608–1674

This is the month, and this the happy morn,
Wherein the Son of Heaven's eternal King,
Of wedded maid and Virgin Mother born,
Our great redemption from above did bring.

JOHN MILTON

J ohn Milton is the best representative of the Puritan spirit in
literature. His imaginative power was tremendous, and next to
Shakespeare, Milton is regarded as the greatest of English poets.

His gifts appeared early; he was already a poet by the age of
ten. At sixteen he attended Christ's College in Cambridge. As
a student, he wrote the companion poems "L'Allegro" (The
Mirthful Man) and "Il Penseroso" (The Serious Man) which, set
to music by Handel, are still universal favorites. Another great
poem coming from this period of his life celebrates the birth of
Christ, "Ode on the Morning of Christ's Nativity."

Recognizing John's great ability, his parents did not force
him to go into law or business, but with rare good judgment
encouraged his interest in literature. The freedom they gave him
at such an early age would have ruined most youths, but not

Milton. A deeply religious young man, he studied the Bible intensely and based his beliefs directly on it. At twenty-three he wrote that he intended to use his talents "as ever in my great Taskmaster's eyes."

Milton's father, an accomplished musician, had made a fortune as a notary and money broker. He supported his son to the age of thirty-two. John could have become a clergyman, but he felt that "tyranny had invaded the church," and so chose to become a poet. Young Milton spent these years studying and writing late into the night, rarely going to bed before midnight.

After his mother died in 1637, Milton toured Europe for fifteen months. He particularly enjoyed Italy for its art, culture, and music, and he had the pleasure of meeting Galileo. Receiving news of mounting political tension in England, he returned home to support the Puritan cause by writing political pamphlets.

After Charles I was beheaded, Oliver Cromwell became head of the Commonwealth. Milton, gifted in several languages, was appointed secretary for foreign languages. He wrote all his letters to other nations in Latin. In these difficult days, he fought not with the sword, but with his pen. These prime years of his life were spent attending to affairs of state, always calling for liberty.

At the age of forty-three, Milton's eyesight failed. His writing and constant studying had taken their toll. But his blindness did not stop him from writing. A well-known painting of Delacroix shows the blind Milton dictating *Paradise Lost* to his daughters.

This great epic poem, describing the war between good and evil, is based on the Bible story of Satan's rebellion against God and the fall of Adam and Eve in the Garden of Eden. *Paradise Regained* shows Christ overcoming Satan's temptations. Milton's great drama *Samson Agonistes* was also dictated by him when totally blind. The incredible fact is that his late, long poems were composed entirely in his mind, especially at night.

One biographer said, "Milton believed that he who would speak worthily of worthy things must himself be a man of lofty virtue." A man of high character, the poet exemplified what he believed. Samuel Johnson said of him, "His studies and meditations were a habitual prayer."

Milton at times devoted himself to writing paraphrases of the Psalms. Those most often sung today are "Let Us, with a Gladsome Mind" and "The Lord Will Come and Not Be Slow." Attracted to Milton's musical poetry, Handel set these paraphrases to music in his *Occasional Oratorio*. Also, Handel's great oratorio *Samson* uses Milton's dramatic poem. Like Milton, Handel was blind in his later years.

His much-tried faith enabled Milton to conquer despair. Never wavering from his trust in God, he found his final authority and comfort in the Bible.

> *For great Thou art, and wonders great*
> *By Thy strong hand are done;*
> *Thou in Thine everlasting seat*
> *Remainest God alone.*

32

James Montgomery
1771–1854

*With the faith of a strong man he
united the simplicity of a child.*

JOHN JULIAN

In James Montgomery's hymns, one hears a newly awakened enthusiasm for evangelizing the world. He was the first English hymn writer to sound the missionary trumpet. His interest in missions came out of a great personal loss. When James was seven, his parents sent him to the Moravian seminary at Fulneck in Yorkshire. Five years later, while James was still at Fulneck, they went as Moravian missionaries to the West Indies. He never saw them again. Both died in the attempt to bring the gospel to poverty-stricken people.

As a result of losing his parents at such an early age, James, like William Cowper, suffered periods of deep depression. He had already begun to write poetry, and he soon felt that he could serve the Lord better as a poet than as a preacher. But the Moravians who were trying to care for the orphan found him to be a dreamer, who "never had a sense of the hour," so they "put him out to business," at least for a time.

He became an assistant to a baker. Finding the work easy, he even had time behind the counter to write verses. One day in a restless mood he packed up and found a similar job in Wath. A year later Montgomery went to London to show some of his poems to publishers, but their total indifference sent him back to Wath, bewildered. After living aimlessly for a time, he started work as an assistant to the printer of a newspaper, *The Sheffield Register*.

Eventually Montgomery took over the paper and edited it for thirty-one years. Never able to forget that his parents had sacrificed their lives ministering to blacks, he became a strong opponent of slavery. Championing the cause of abolition and other controversial causes in the pages of his paper landed him in prison twice. Many of his poems in the book, *Prison Amusements*, were written from a jail cell.

Although Montgomery was a voluminous writer, producing many poems as well as prose, only his hymns have had the enduring quality to live on. With his extensive biblical knowledge and an ear for rhythm that was accurate and refined, he was one of the great layman hymn writers of the church. Some of his best-known are "Stand Up and Bless the Lord," "Hail to the Lord's Anointed," and "Angels, from the Realms of Glory."

Montgomery's last words were words of prayer. It was the time of his usual evening devotions. Soon afterward he died, fulfilling the thought contained in his precious hymn:

> *Prayer is the Christian's vital breath,*
> *The Christian's native air,*
> *His watchword at the gates of death;*
> *He enters heaven with prayer.*

33

John Mason Neale
1818–1866

*He was admired for his vast industry,
his rigid consistency, his patience
under long adversity, and his heroic,
unflinching faith.*

PHILIP SCHAFF

L ike so many other eminent men and women in history, John
Mason Neale received the greater part of his early education
from his gifted, learned mother. He was five when his father died.
Educated at Trinity College, Cambridge, he became noted for his
prolific writing of prose and received numerous prizes for his poetry.

Neale combined in his personality a happy mixture of gentleness and firmness—a lovable person with strong convictions.
Possessing great and varied talents, he was an excellent scholar. He
steeped his mind in medieval Latin and knew eighteen or nineteen other languages. His time was divided between excessive literary toil and exhausting labors of piety and benevolence.

For about twenty years, until his death, he served as warden
of Sackville College in East Grimstead. Actually an almshouse for
a few old people, the school paid him a minimal salary but also
demanded little of his time, so he did not mind. The schedule

gave him time to continue his literary work. Though a renowned ecclesiastical historian, he is best remembered as a hymnologist, and he has had an enormous influence on modern hymnody.

Through his translations, Neale did more than any other person to make available the rich heritage of Greek and Latin hymns. His book *Hymns of the Eastern Church* opened up a mine of treasures to Christendom. He traveled in Eastern countries, and by going through Greece, he caught the spirit of the Greek hymns. Often his translations read like original poems, such as this verse from the Greek:

> *Art thou weary, art thou languid?*
> *Art thou sore distressed?*
> *"Come to me," saith One, "and, coming,*
> *Be at rest."*

Neale often suffered from poor health and wore himself out with his arduous labors. He died before the age of fifty, trusting in the atoning blood of Christ.

> *All glory, laud and honor*
> *To Thee, Redeemer, King*
> *To whom the lips of children*
> *Made sweet hosannas ring:*
> *Thou art the King of Israel,*
> *Thou David's royal Son,*
> *Who in the Lord's name comest,*
> *The King and blessed One!*

34

John Newton
1725–1807

How sweet the name of Jesus sounds
In a believer's ear!
It soothes his sorrows,
heals his wounds,
And drives away his fear.

JOHN NEWTON

John Newton described himself as a wretch; some biographers have used the word *wild*. Newton had to go through incredible suffering before he came to the end of himself and his headstrong nature was mastered by One stronger than he.

Newton knew little of his sea captain father, a severe man who was usually away in the Mediterranean. John's mother found her greatest joy in teaching her only son hymns, passages from the Bible, and the catechism. She hoped he would enter the ministry, but she died when he was only seven. With his father at sea and his mother gone, he had to shift for himself.

He went to school only from age eight to ten. Then he fell in with the wrong friends and began reading atheistic literature. His life became increasingly dissolute.

At the age of eleven he joined his father's ship. Five years later when the ship was in port, a press gang jumped him and forced him to sail on a British man-of-war. As soon as he could, he tried to desert the English navy; however, he was captured, publicly flogged, and reduced in rank.

The one restraining influence on his reckless life at sea was his faithful love for Mary Catlett. He had first met her when he was seventeen and she fourteen. Only the thought of one day marrying her saved him from drowning himself in despair.

At length he became the servant of an unscrupulous slave-trader off the coast of Sierra Leone. His cruel master put him through a terrible time of hardship and degradation. He nearly starved to death, but the slaves in their chains pitied him and secretly gave him of their scanty food.

Eventually Newton escaped. When the ship on which he sailed began to founder in a terrifying storm, he remembered his mother's prayers. He cried out to God for help and repented of his evil ways. The John Newton who arrived safely in England was a new man in Christ Jesus.

After his marriage to Mary in 1750, he continued to make voyages as the commander of a slave ship. In his leisure time he studied mathematics, French, and Latin. Eventually, the inhuman nature of the slave trade began to dawn on Newton, mostly due to the influence of William Wilberforce. Finally, Newton quit the sea in 1755 and became tide-surveyor in Liverpool.

He continued to study the Scriptures in Greek and Hebrew. Influenced by the preaching of the Wesleys and Whitefield, Newton applied to the Archbishop of York for holy orders in 1758. He was refused. Finally at the age of thirty-nine, he was offered the curacy at Olney through the influence of a friend. While he served there, he was ordained a minister.

William Cowper settled in the parish at the urging of Newton, and they became close friends. They spent four days of each week together, collaborating on the "Olney hymns" (1779) for the Tuesday evening prayer meetings. These hymns are one of the most important contributions to evangelical hymnody.

When his eyesight and health began to fail, his friends suggested he stop preaching. "What," he exclaimed, "shall the old African blasphemer stop while he can still speak?" He was still preaching at nearly eighty years old, but he was so fragile a friend stood in the pulpit with him to help him read his sermons. One Sunday he read twice the words, "Jesus Christ is precious."

The assistant whispered, "You have already said that twice."

Newton turned to his helper and said, "Yes, I said that twice, and I'm going to say it again." For the third time the old preacher said loudly, "Jesus Christ is precious!"*

Among his many hymns, "Amazing Grace," a testimony of Newton's early life and conversion continues to be sung with enthusiasm, joy, and tears.

> *Amazing grace! how sweet the sound,*
> *That saved a wretch like me!*
> *I once was lost, but now am found,*
> *Was blind, but now I see.*

---

*From E. E. Ryden, *The Story of Christian Hymnody* (Rock Island, IL: Augustana Press, 1959).

35

Ray Palmer
1808–1887

Lowell Mason
1792–1872

*Palmer's whole life was characterized
by a warm devotion to Christ.*

E. E. RYDEN

Because of financial difficulties, Ray Palmer had to leave
school at the age of thirteen and go to work. He found a job
as a clerk in a Boston dry goods store, and for the two years he
spent there, he went through a number of spiritual struggles. In
the end he became a Christian. Later he was able to complete his
education and eventually graduate from Yale.

In the following year, he constantly battled two enemies—
illness and loneliness. As with many of the hymn writers, he
found comfort in writing a poem. This poem became the precious hymn, "My Faith Looks Up to Thee." He was only twenty-
two when he wrote it and had no thought that it would become
a great hymn that would continue to be sung by people around
the world. Today it is considered one of America's finest. Lowell
Mason, who wrote the music, said to Palmer, "You may live many

years and do many good things, but I think you will be best known to posterity as the author of 'My Faith Looks Up to Thee.'"

Palmer was the first American writer to translate Latin hymns into English. His translation of the hymn of Bernard of Clairvaux, "Jesus Thou Joy of Loving Hearts," is a gem of rare beauty.

He also took an active interest in education and literature, was successful in the ministry, and wrote for leading religious papers. But Mason was right—Palmer is best known for "My Faith Looks Up to Thee."

Lowell Mason is considered one of America's greatest hymn tune composers. He wrote the music for "Nearer, My God, to Thee," "When I Survey the Wondrous Cross," and "O Day of Rest and Gladness." According to Gilbert Chase in *America's Music*, "His role in the development of music education in America cannot be overestimated." Perhaps as an indication of his importance, he has been referred to as the Father of American church and public school music.

> *My faith looks up to Thee,*
> *Thou Lamb of Calvary,*
> *Savior divine!*
> *Now hear me while I pray,*
> *Take all my guilt away,*
> *O let me from this day*
> *Be wholly Thine!*

36

Elizabeth P. Prentiss

1818–1878

It is remarkable how many of David's psalms date from those dark and sad days when he was hunted as a partridge upon the mountains.

F. B. MEYER

E lizabeth Payson Prentiss grew up in a happy home in Portland, Maine. Her father, the Reverend Edward Payson, not only taught the truth of the Bible, but modeled the Christian life so well that many years after his death numerous children were still being named for him.

Elizabeth exhibited unusual gifts as a writer from childhood. When she was sixteen, she was already contributing verses and articles to a magazine. She taught school for a number of years, and in 1845 married the Reverend George L. Prentiss. He later became a professor at Union Theological Seminary in New York. They had two children.

Those who knew Elizabeth described her as a "bright-eyed little lady with a keen sense of humor." She preferred to be home most of the time rather than going to meetings and social gatherings. Throughout most of her life she scarcely knew what it meant to be without pain. She suffered particularly from headaches and chronic insomnia. Because she would rather make people happy than tell them all her problems, she rarely mentioned her condition.

Elizabeth wrote a successful book called *Stepping Heavenward*. Her purpose in writing it was to strengthen and comfort others. She also gained recognition as a poet and hymn writer. But soon, as E. E. Ryden relates in *The Story of Christian Hymnody*, her faith was destined to undergo an even greater trial than aches and pains.

Shortly after the family moved to New York City, the Prentisses lost their oldest child. Then tragedy struck another hammer blow—their other child died. One evening when the sad parents returned home after putting flowers on the graves of their children, Elizabeth cried out in anguish, "Our home is broken up, our lives wrecked, our hopes shattered, our dreams dissolved. Sometimes I don't think I can stand living for another moment, much less a lifetime."

Her husband held her in his arms and let her cry. Then in a quiet voice, he said just the thing to help her turn back to the only source of comfort in this sad world: "In times like these, God loves us all the more, just as we loved our children in their distress."

Shortly after this conversation, her husband was called upon to help someone in the neighborhood. Elizabeth picked up her Bible and hymnal and went to her room. She read a number of passages from Scripture, and then turned to the hymnbook to find words of comfort and consolation. She stopped at Sarah

Adams's "Nearer My God to Thee" and read it several times. She began to think about that moment in history when God met Jacob in a time of human sorrow and need, and bowed her head praying that she might have a similar experience.

As she was praying, these words came to her mind: "More love to Thee, O Christ, more love to Thee. . . ." It is interesting that her hymn is in the same metrical pattern as "Nearer My God to Thee."

Not even Elizabeth's husband knew about her hymn until thirteen years after its writing. The first printing of "More Love to Thee, O Christ" was on a leaflet. Soon it was being sung throughout the country at revival meetings. The melody was written by William Doane, the manufacturer, who wrote many other fine hymn tunes.

Elizabeth Prentiss died in 1878. She was mourned around the world. Even a message came from China—with a fan on which were the words of her beautiful hymn in Chinese characters.

> *More love to thee, O Christ!*
> *More love to thee!*
> *Hear thou the prayer I make,*
> *On bended knee;*
> *This is my earnest plea,*
> *More love, O Christ, to thee,*
> *More love to thee! More love to thee!*

37

Christina Rossetti
1830–1894

For he who much has suffered,
much will know.

HOMER

L ong before Christina Rossetti was twenty, she was writing
verses about all that she found most beautiful in nature and
in her imagination. Yet another part of her brilliant mind was
chanting *vanitas vanitatum*. That might sound like a contradic-
tion, but she saw life from a Christian perspective. She recognized the beauty, wonder, and variety that coexist in the world
with suffering, hardships, and a multitude of unexplained difficulties.

Even though Christina lived much of her life with little
money, poor health, and unattained goals (she was engaged twice
but never married because of religious differences), she developed an amazing serenity and cheerfulness. Particularly later in
life, she exhibited considerable down-to-earth common sense
and humor. This can only be explained by her Christian faith, as

she experienced a succession of serious illnesses. While these trials inclined her to melancholy, they did not hinder her creativity nor interrupt her writing. Beneath the humility and quiet, saintly life which others saw lay a passionate Italian temperament.

Christina, her sister, and two brothers were educated at home by their mother, who had been a governess before her marriage. Mrs. Rossetti had a strong faith in God. She read to her children from the Bible, St. Augustine, and *Pilgrim's Progress*. She taught them the catechism and introduced them to many other books that broadened their outlook. *The Arabian Nights* was one of Christina's favorites.

A highly cultured woman of English and Italian background, Mrs. Rossetti had an interest in writing poetry. She was deeply loved by her children and was the delight of Christina's heart. Many of Christina's poems were dedicated to her. Once her mother said whimsically, "I have never received a valentine from anyone." Each year afterwards Christina not only gave her mother a valentine, but also included an original poem.

The father was also a poet. A political refugee from Italy, he became a professor of Italian at Kings College, Oxford. He was a Dante scholar and could quote the entire *Divine Comedy* from memory.

This remarkable family lived in various dingy homes in the Bloomsbury area of London, surrounded by Italian exiles and English artists. In this exciting atmosphere, the parents and children often spent their evenings in front of the parlor fireplace discussing literature, especially the Italian classics, and painting. Consequently Christina, her sister, and two brothers all became writers. Brother Dante Gabriel also gained recognition as a painter.

When Christina was twelve, her grandfather published some of her first poems. They already prefigured the richness of her vision. At age twenty she submitted some poems to the Pre-Raphaelite journal, *The Germ*. They appeared under the pseudonym Ellen Alleyn. The Pre-Raphaelites, a group formed in 1848 under the influence of Ruskin, greatly stimulated Christina. Her two brothers, Holman Hunt, Millais, and later Burne-Jones, Morris, and others were active in the movement. Formed primarily to exchange ideas, the Pre-Raphaelites encouraged painting with the fidelity to nature and delicacy of treatment characteristic of Italian art before the time of Raphael. Their ideal was "true to nature." Christina spent much time with these imaginative, hardworking people, and from time to time posed as their model, especially for Dante Gabriel Rossetti's paintings of the Virgin Mary.

When the father's health began to fail, Mrs. Rossetti gave French and Italian lessons so the family would have some income. Christina was supposed to train to be a governess, but poor health prevented her. Her brother William, who had prospered sufficiently to buy a home, invited the family to live with him soon after the father died. Christina was financially dependent on her brother for many years. She was thankful, but still found it hard to accept. She already had had a life plagued with hesitations and postponements. In the poem "Another Spring," she described her dependent condition as a stinging comment on her life. However in the words of one critic, "Her buoyant and tender soul was sharpened and refined by blow after blow of harsh discipline."

> *If I might see another Spring,*
> *I'd not plant summer flowers and wait,*
> *I'd have my crocuses at once . . .*
> *Leaf-nested primroses; anything*
> *To blow at once, not late . . . .*
> *If I might see another Spring,*
> *I'd laugh today, today is brief;*
> *I would not wait for anything:*
> *I'd use today that cannot last,*
> *Be glad today and sing.*

Urged by her brother Dante Gabriel to prepare a volume of poetry that he would illustrate, she published the book *Goblin Market and Other Poems* in 1862. She was at once proclaimed a poet of charm, originality, and brilliance. *Goblin Market* remains her most famous single poem. In 1872 Christina wrote *Sing-Song*, a much loved collection of nursery rhymes for children.

Today when so much literature is filled with doubt, denial, and misery, the writings of Christina Rossetti are a message to our minds and hearts. To the end of her career, Dante and the Bible with commentaries continued to be the backbone of her reading. Whenever she was able, she occupied herself with church work.

Several of her poems have become Christmas carols. "In the Bleak Mid-Winter" describes the nativity scene in terms of the chilly English countryside. It is set to exquisite music by the noted English composer, Gustav Holst. Another of her lovely Christmas songs is "Love Came Down at Christmas."

In 1871 Christina was stricken with Grave's disease, which affected her appearance and endangered her life. She accepted her affliction with Christian courage and resignation and lived another twenty-three years using what energy she had mainly for devotional writing.

By the late nineteenth century, Christina's works were being compared to Elizabeth Barrett Browning's. Today "Christina Rossetti's poetry is more widely read and of keener interest to readers and critics than ever before," said biographer Eleanor Walter Thomas.

This fact would be astonishing to the timid, modest Christina who "deprecated getting into paragraphs." Even when she was dying, she asked her church to pray for her but not to mention her name.

In her lifetime she wrote over nine hundred poems in English and sixty in Italian. The majority of them are religious in subject and mood. Some of her books are a combination of poetry and prose, with simple but thought-provoking titles, such as *Called to Be Saints, Time Flies,* and *Seek and Find.*

Among the foremost poets of her time, Christina Rossetti made Christ the main focus of her life. She defines her faith in her beautiful hymn, "None Other Lamb":

> *None other Lamb, none other name,*
> *None other hope in heaven or earth or sea,*
> *None other hiding-place from guilt and shame,*
> *None beside Thee.*

My faith burns low, my hope burns low;
Only my heart's desire cries out in me
By the deep thunder of its want and woe,
Cries out to Thee.
Lord, Thou art Life, though I be dead;
Love's fire Thou art, however cold I be:
Nor heav'n have I, nor place to lay my head,
Nor home, but Thee.

38

Lina Sandell

1832–1903

The church owes many of her
sweetest hymns to the profound
anguish which wrung the hearts
of her noblest children.

F. B. MEYER

The nineteenth century witnessed the phenomenon of women assuming a place of primary importance among hymn writers of the church. England had Charlotte Elliott, Frances Havergal, and Christina Rossetti. America had Fanny Crosby and Anna Warner. Sweden had Lina Sandell. Gifted women hymn writers appeared simultaneously with the great spiritual revivals which swept over Europe and America in successive tidal waves from 1800 to 1875.

Frail as a child, Lina Sandell preferred spending time in her father's study to playing outdoors with her friends. She learned two important things from her father, the pastor in Froderyd—the hope one has when one believes the Bible and the helpfulness of learning to study in a methodical way. Tutored by her father and her brother-in-law, she received a good liberal arts education as well as training in the interpretation of the Scriptures.

When she was twelve, she was stricken with a severe illness that left her with paralysis. The physician pronounced her case hopeless. But one day when everyone else was in church, she prayed and asked the Lord to help her get up out of bed. She dressed herself and very slowly walked across the room. She could hardly wait for her parents to come home and see what the Lord had done in answer to all their prayers.

The experience filled her heart with a deep sense of gratitude and love for the Lord that no later sorrows or trouble could shake. She began to write down her thoughts, and a small book of poems was published when she was sixteen.

About ten years later, she accompanied her father on a visit to Gothenberg. As they were crossing Lake Vattern, the small boat gave a sudden lurch. The two of them were standing by a railing, and her father fell overboard and drowned before her eyes.

The tragedy caused Lina deep and extended anguish, but out of this sorrow came some of her finest hymns. She comforted herself and others with the everlasting hope she had learned from Scripture. Even though God did bring good out of this experience, Lina went through a sad, restless time for three years. In her diary she confessed her impatient and unloving spirit towards members of her own family and prayed constantly that the Lord would heal the illness and despair of her soul.

When she was thirty-five, Lina married C. O. Berg. It was a good marriage, but there were tensions too. As my friend, Miss

Smith, wisely said the other day, "Getting along with people is never easy, but getting along without them is impossible."

Lina Sandell lived to write about 650 hymns. One of the earliest was "Children of the Heavenly Father." This hymn was sung not only in Sweden, but the Swedish emigrants who sailed to America came singing it. It was a source of comfort and strength in the midst of the troubles and difficulties of settling into a new land and leaving behind relatives and friends.

The remarkable popularity of her hymns was due in part to the melodies written by Oscar Ahnfelt, an enthusiastic and gifted musician. Ahnfelt became known as the "Swedish troubadour" in a time of revival under preacher Carl Rosenius. Ahnfelt went about Sweden playing his ten-stringed guitar and singing hymns.

God worked through the association between Ahnfelt, Rosenius, and Sandell in an unusual way. Carl Rosenius had been brought up in a Christian home, but while he was a student at Upsala University, his faith was severely shaken. Professors and students alike acted as if truth did not exist.

At this time, an English minister named George Scott began preaching in Stockholm. It was the beginning of revival in Sweden, and Carl Rosenius found what he was seeking—confirmation that the Bible is trustworthy. He, in turn, became the spiritual inspiration to many people including Oscar Ahnfelt and singer Jenny Lind.

According to E. E. Ryden (*The Story of Christian Hymnody*), Rosenius and Ahnfelt encountered much opposition in their evangelistic ministry. At one time the king of Sweden was asked to forbid Ahnfelt's preaching and singing. The king said, "First I must hear the 'spiritual troubadour.'"

Greatly concerned about this meeting, Ahnfelt asked Lina Sandell to write a special hymn for the occasion. She wrote "Who Is It That Knocketh?" and while Ahnfelt sang it, the king listened with moist eyes. Afterward he exclaimed, "You may sing as much as you desire in both of my kingdoms!"

As there was no money to print the hymns of Sandell and Ahnfelt, Jenny Lind assisted financially with the first collection of twelve songs. Lina said later, "Ahnfelt has sung my songs into the hearts of the people."

Jenny Lind, the "Swedish Nightingale," not only saw that the hymns were put into print, but at revival meetings she would join her marvelous voice with those of the working people sitting on rough benches, singing the hymns of Lina Sandell. Lind had given up her brilliant opera career because of her Christian convictions. She offered her testimony to the Lord largely through Lina's hymns.

Jenny Lind influenced many people. In his book *Hans Christian Andersen*, Elias Bredsdorff reported that Andersen once claimed that it was through Jenny Lind he first became sensible of the holiness there is in art; through her he learned that one must forget one's self in the service of the Supreme.

For nearly forty years, Lina Sandell helped to edit the *Korsblomman*. It was a yearly volume of stories, poems, biographies, and devotional pieces. One issue had an allegory about an old clock that had suddenly stopped ticking. The dial discovered that the pendulum was at fault.

The pendulum explained, "I'm tired of swinging back and forth 86,400 times each day."

"Try swinging six times only," suggested the dial.

"Oh, you're right, that's not hard to do," the pendulum said, "but it's not six times, or sixty; it's the thought of six million times that disturbs me."

The dial reflected and came up with this helpful idea: "Bear in mind, Sir, that while in a single moment you can think of the millions of swings you must make in a lifetime, only one swing at a time will be required of you."

The pendulum thanked the dial for his sound advice and promptly resumed his work.

Lina Sandell, in commenting on the allegory, said that it is foolish to put future burdens upon the present moment.

"We are given one day at a time," she said, "and for each day, new grace, new strength, new help."

On the opposite page to the story about the clock was printed her hymn:

> *Day by day, and with each passing moment,*
> *Strength I find to meet my trials here;*
> *Trusting in my Father's wise bestowment,*
> *I've no cause for worry or for fear.*

A well-known writer in Sweden said recently that every Swede ought to begin each day with this hymn. Happily it is translated into many other languages also.

In spite of her fragile health, Lina Sandell lived to be seventy-one. At her funeral the choir sang "Children of the

Heavenly Father," and the congregation joined in spontaneously. Ten thousand people gathered in the parsonage yard in Froderyd in 1953 for the dedication of a bronze statue in her memory. The little cottage where she lived for a time is now a museum.

Those of us with a Swedish background will always consider "Children of the Heavenly Father" one of our favorite hymns.

> *Children of the heavenly Father*
> *Safely in His bosom gather;*
> *Nestling bird nor star in heaven*
> *Such a refuge e'er was given.*
> *Neither life nor death shall ever*
> *From the Lord His children sever;*
> *Unto them His grace He showeth,*
> *And their sorrows all He knoweth.*
> *Though He giveth or He taketh,*
> *God His children ne'er forsaketh;*
> *His the loving purpose solely*
> *To preserve them pure and holy.*

39

Joseph Scriven
1819–1886

*I have called you friends, for everything
that I learned from my Father I have
made known to you.*

JOHN 15:15

On the day before Joseph Scriven was to marry the young woman who shared his ideals and hopes in life, she accidentally drowned in a pool of water. The shock shattered his life, and in a sense he never recovered from this tragic event.

In 1845 at the age of twenty-five Scriven moved to Canada. He spent the remainder of his life helping the poor. At different times he lived with friends—sometimes as a guest and other times as a teacher. He helped to repair homes for the needy and sawed wood so they could keep their cottages warm throughout the long Canadian winters. It was typical of him to give away his own clothes to someone who had less. There were those who considered the Irishman queer—an eccentric. Many Christians have received a similar label.

When he was in his late thirties, he learned that his mother back in Ireland was seriously ill, mentally and physically. Because of his poverty, he had no way to go to her, but he did what he could. He wrote a loving letter and enclosed a hymn he had written. The opening lines read:

> *What a friend we have in Jesus,*
> *All our sins and griefs to bear;*
> *What a privilege to carry*
> *Everything to God in prayer!*

So modest was Joseph Scriven about his giftedness that his hymn was only discovered "accidentally." No one knew he had a gift for writing poems or hymns. (A music critic has said that imagination makes poems; devotion makes hymns. Thus it seems more correct to speak of "What a Friend We Have in Jesus" as a hymn rather than as a poem, although no music had been written for it at this time.)

About five years after his mother's illness, Scriven grew sick himself. A friend who called on him discovered the hymn. With joy the neighbor read the words and learned the circumstances which prompted Scriven to write his one and only hymn. Later, whenever anyone would ask him how he wrote it, Scriven would answer, "The Lord and I did it together."

No one knows exactly how the hymn found its way to Richmond, Virginia, but in 1870 it was printed there in a Sunday school songbook. About five years later it came to the attention of song leader Ira D. Sankey who, with Philip P. Bliss, was in the process of preparing *Gospel Hymns No. 1*. They had already chosen a hymn (both words and music) by the well-known composer

Charles C. Converse, but they decided to substitute Scriven's lyrics. Sankey said later, "Thus the last hymn that went into the book became one of the first in favor." The tune by Converse was the right choice for this hymn.

As one critic has said, "The very simplicity of both words and music has perhaps been the strength and charm of the song." Many love the hymn because of its assurance of Jesus' commitment to the believer. This hymn is often one of the first missionaries teach their converts.

Near Lake Ontario beside the highway running north from Port Hope to Peterborough stands a monument with this inscription: "Four Miles North in Pengelly's Cemetery/Lies the Philanthropist/And Author of the Great Masterpiece/Written at Port Hope, 1857." Then follows the three stanzas of "What a Friend We Have in Jesus."

Scriven's story is a great encouragement. His life did not work out the way he had planned. He must have battled with disappointment and loneliness, but he looked to his Friend and shared His love with widows and poor folk. We do not have to do great exploits to be remembered in this world and the next.

Have we trials and temptations?
Is there trouble anywhere?
We should never be discouraged.
Take it to the Lord in prayer.
Can we find a friend so faithful,
Who will all our sorrows share?
Jesus knows our every weakness;
Take it to the Lord in prayer.

40

Harriet Beecher Stowe
1811–1896

Genius is nothing else than a
great aptitude for patience.

GEORGES BUFFON

Harriet Beecher Stowe is best known for her novel, *Uncle Tom's Cabin*, but she also wrote hymns that deserve a place in the best collections. Dr. E. E. Ryden, in his excellent book *The Story of Christian Hymnody*, said, "For sheer poetic beauty there is probably not a single American lyric that can excel 'Still, Still with Thee.'" This hymn is based on Psalm 139:18.

A multitalented woman like Harriet Beecher Stowe does not just wake up one morning and start to write hymns that are helpful to thousands of people. It takes years of learning and living through hard experiences to make one sympathetic to others. And it takes patience, patience, patience.

It is true, she had an amazing background. Her father was the most powerful Puritan preacher of his generation in the United States, having been influenced by Jonathan Edwards. Her mother, a devout Christian, died before Harriet was four years old.

When Mrs. Beecher was dying, her last prayer was that her six sons might be called to the ministry. The prayer was answered in years to come. The youngest son, Henry Ward Beecher, became the greatest preacher of his time.

We do not know what Mrs. Beecher prayed for her daughter, Harriet, but we do know that Harriet became the author of one of America's all-time bestsellers, plus many other works. In 1896 her collected writings were published in sixteen volumes.

Harriet had a bright mind with a remarkable memory. When she was six, she could read well and had memorized over twenty-five hymns and two long chapters from the Bible. She was sent to a private school where her father taught the Bible and accordingly received free tuition for his children. Her sister, Catherine, began her own school a few years later. Harriet was first a pupil and later a member of the faculty. She was an avid reader and especially liked Sir Walter Scott and Lord Byron.

In 1836 she married Dr. Calvin Stowe, a professor and leading authority on the Bible. He had a fine sense of humor, which matched her own, but unfortunately his health was fragile.

Though Harriet had become a Christian as a young girl, she had many conflicts between faith and doubt after she married. Her questions arose due to a series of misfortunes and sorrows. Her sixth child, a particular favorite of hers, died of cholera. At the same time, her husband was in a sanatorium because of poor health, which left him depressed; so all the problems and anxieties of running the home fell upon her shoulders.

In a letter to her husband, she describes the cholera plague raging in Cincinnati. "This week has been unusually fatal," she wrote. "Hearse drivers have scarce been allowed to unharness their horses, while furniture carts and other vehicles are often employed for the removal of the dead . . ." (from *The Story of Christian Hymnody* by E. E. Ryden).

Her hymn "Still, Still with Thee" was written not long after her son Charles died. Then other family tragedies occurred. Their eldest son, Henry, was drowned at the close of his freshman year at Dartmouth, and their third son, Fred, was wounded at Gettysburg and left mentally impaired afterwards.

Through all this grief, her basic faith in the Lord was firm, even though she had times of bewilderment. Because of her husband's poor health, there wasn't enough money to pay bills. Harriet began to write articles for a magazine, the *National Era*. Writing was not exactly easy, as she was a devoted mother and had much to do in their home.

Around the time when she began to write, she became interested in the "underground railway" which helped runaway slaves reach the Canadian border. She became deeply involved in the plight of these poor people and wished someone would do something to help them.

One day she received a letter from her sister-in-law, Isabella. "Hattie," she said, "if I could use a pen as you can, I would write something that will make this whole nation feel what an accursed thing slavery is."

Harriet replied, "As long as the baby sleeps with me nights, I can't do much . . . but I shall do it at last" (from *Life and Letters of Harriet Beecher Stowe* by Annie Fields).

Finally, she began writing her story in serial form for the

National Era, but not without interruptions. Various family members came to visit, and Harriet, in an effort to find privacy, often used the kitchen table as her desk. Her sister Catherine saw that Harriet could not go on with her writing unless she had some freedom, so she offered to spend one year in the Stowe household helping out.

Scarcely had the last installment appeared in the *National Era* when a Boston publisher wanted to print it in book form. With its publication in 1852, Harriet Beecher Stowe became one of the most famous women in the world. *Uncle Tom's Cabin* had a profound influence on the American people and probably affected the course of the Civil War.

Within a short time, her book was translated into many languages. During its first year in print, more than a million and a half copies circulated in Britain and its colonies. On a trip to Europe, Harriet met Kingsley, Ruskin, Dickens, and other members of the English literary set.

In 1852 Charles Dickens wrote that he considered *Uncle Tom's Cabin* a noble work, lofty humanity, the gentlest, sweetest, and yet boldest writing. He also mentioned that her masterpiece was not free from the fault of overstrained conclusions and violent extremes. This observation is particularly humorous for those of us who love Dickens and read and reread his books all the time, because his books definitely share this weakness.

Later Harriet carried on a correspondence with George Eliot. In America she became friends with Oliver Wendell Holmes and Mark Twain.

E. E. Ryden reports that in the year following the publication of Harriet's work, Jenny Lind came to the United States to earn money to found a musical academy for talented girls in Stockholm. She too was very impressed with Mrs. Stowe and wrote her, "I have the feeling about *Uncle Tom's Cabin* that great changes will take place by and by and that the writer of that book can fall asleep today or tomorrow with the bright, sweet consciousness of having been a strong means in the Creator's hand of having accomplished essential good."

One of Harriet Beecher Stowe's biographers said that to read *Uncle Tom's Cabin* is a necessary part of one's education, important for understanding the way the past has affected today's society. It is one of the most influential books ever published.

As we go from crisis to crisis in the last few years of the twentieth century, we need to pray for another Harriet Beecher Stowe to bring forth a book with the force and spiritual message to awaken us to our need for revival and reformation.

Still, still with thee, when purple morning breaketh,
When the bird waketh and the shadows flee;
Fairer than morning, lovelier than the daylight,
Dawns the sweet consciousness, I am with thee.
So shall it be at last, in that bright morning
When the soul waketh and life's shadows flee:
O, in that hour, fairer than daylight dawning,
Shall rise the glorious thought, I am with thee.

41

Augustus M. Toplady
1740–1778

For the Lord God is
an everlasting rock—
the Rock of ages.

ISAIAH 26:4 (*Amplified Bible*)

Augustus M. Toplady was born in Farnham, England. His father, a British army major, was killed in the war and never saw his son. His mother, a woman of strong character and deep piety, placed Augustus at Westminster School in London where such outstanding hymn writers as Charles Wesley, William Cowper, and John Dryden had graduated. Toplady had a deep sense of appreciation and love for his mother, who planned his education wisely.

When the family moved to Ireland, he attended Trinity College in Dublin, graduating in 1760. At age sixteen Toplady attended a religious meeting held in a barn. The lay preacher "could hardly spell his name," but his message awakened the student searching for truth. Augustus was converted that day, but it was another three years before he saw clearly the great goodness of God.

Later when Toplady became a curate, he was taking a walk one afternoon. A severe thunderstorm blew up, and he found an opening in an immense granite rock, ran into it, and watched the storm from this shelter. Thoughts of Christ as a sheltering rock took hold of his mind, and he began to form the words for the great hymn of faith, "Rock of Ages."

This hymn has been an enormous comfort to people caught in the storms of life. General J. E. B. Stuart, the famous Confederate cavalry leader, was mortally wounded at Yellow Tavern, VA. As he lay dying in a Richmond hospital, he called for his minister and asked that "Rock of Ages" be sung to him.

Toplady was a contemporary of John Wesley, and for many years they were rather unpleasant to each other. Toplady, a confirmed Calvinist, was intolerant of Wesley's Arminian views. However, in the year that Toplady wrote "Rock of Ages," he brought out a collection of hymns and psalms by numerous writers. Despite his bitter controversy with John Wesley, he included in his book a large number of Wesley's hymns.

As Toplady lay dying he exclaimed, "I enjoy heaven already in my soul. My prayers are all converted into praises." Although he was only thirty-eight, his end was jubilant and triumphant.

> *Rock of Ages, cleft for me,*
> *Let me hide myself in Thee;*
> *Let the water and the blood,*
> *From Thy riven side which flowed,*
> *Be of sin the double cure,*
> *Cleanse me from its guilt and power.*

42

Anna Bartlett Warner
1820–1915

*In a good hymn you have to be simple and
practical. The moment you cease to be
commonplace and put in any expression out
of the common, it ceases to be a hymn.*

ALFRED, LORD TENNYSON

One Sunday at the close of a church service at Swiss L'Abri, Francis Schaeffer asked the congregation to sing, "Jesus Loves Me, This I Know." He smiled and added, "Some of you may realize that this is my favorite hymn."

As we sang this children's hymn together, many of us became aware of how needful it is for songs to have simple, direct words that penetrate our hearts. "Yes, Jesus loves me, the Bible tells me so."

Later in the afternoon when some students dropped by our chalet to say good-bye, one young man from Oxford said, "I would have thought that an intellectual like Dr. Schaeffer, so often involved in long, intense theological and philosophical discussions, would have been drawn to the great hymn writers of the past, like St. Ambrose or Martin Luther."

But over the years, Francis Schaeffer learned that while many of the people he talked with (often for hours) needed intellectual answers to their questions, they also needed a direct message to their hearts. Anna Bartlett Warner's hymn, "Jesus Loves Me," conveys a certainty of scriptural truth that leads to peace, joy, and freedom.

The Warner sisters, Anna and Susan, spent their early years in New York City. Their father, a prosperous lawyer, bought Constitution Island on the Hudson River for a summer home; but he lost heavily in the panic of 1837, and the old house on the island became the family home.

The sisters, eager to do something to earn money so they could go on living on the island, turned to writing. Susan's *Wide, Wide World* was a great success, and her second novel, *Queechy*, nearly equaled it. Anna's *Dollars and Sense* and her other stories for young people sold moderately well over a long period.

But Anna's real interest in life was writing hymns. She edited two hymnbooks. "Jesus Loves Me" was first published in the second hymnbook, *Original Hymns*, but it actually came from her novel, *Say and Seal* (1859). This is undoubtedly the best-known hymn in the world. It has been translated into more languages than any other song. Missionaries have found it one of their best means of explaining the gospel in a clear, simple way to those who speak a very different language.

When Mao Tse-tung founded the People's Republic in 1949, the church in China went through severe persecution. Friends in America received scarcely any news from the Chinese Christians, but in 1972 came a message with this unusual sentence, "The 'This I Know' people are well."

The authorities who censored the mail thought it nonsense and let the letter pass, but Christians brought up on Anna Warner's hymn were immediately comforted to hear that their friends were all right.

There are many stories related to this hymn. A young man born in Winnipeg told about how he would sometimes go with a Canadian trapper into the wilderness. "As our snowshoes went swiftly over the glistening whiteness, Pierre always sang the same song, sometimes in French, sometimes in Eskimo. I liked it and asked him to teach me the words. He did, in the Eskimo language. I asked, 'Where did you pick that up?'

"'O,' he said, 'at the mission.'"

It was, of course, "Jesus Loves Me, This I Know."

Amy Carmichael, the great Irish missionary, founded Dohnavur Fellowship in India, a work that has had a lasting influence on L'Abri Fellowship. She spoke of an experience she had at Marlborough House in Yorkshire, England. She referred to it as "the one watered moment in an arid three years."

One night she attended a special children's mission meeting where Edwin Arrowsmith spoke. She said that she had no recollection of what he said, but the words of Anna Warner's hymn, "Jesus Loves Me," helped her to understand something she had not comprehended before. All her life she had heard of Jesus' love, but she realized now at the age of fifteen that she had never "opened the door" to the Lord. She said of that night that the Good Shepherd in His great mercy answered the prayers of her mother and father and many other loving ones and drew her into His fold. It is interesting to note that Amy Carmichael later wrote many hymns.

Anna Warner's poem early became associated with the tune Bradbury provided for it in one of his collections of hymns, *The Golden Shower* (1862). Both text and tune retain a certain child-like simplicity which has saved them from the fate of untold numbers of contemporary Sunday school songs.

For more than fifty years, the Warner sisters devoted their Sunday afternoons to conducting a Bible class for the cadets who came from all parts of the United States to be trained at West Point. Their man of all work, Buckner, would row the flat-bottomed boat to the dock where the holders of tickets waited to be ferried. After the lesson, followed by tea and gingerbread, Buckner would row them safely home again. Susan was the teacher until her death in 1885, when Anna took her place. Anna lived to be ninety-five years old. Military honors were accorded to both sisters when they died. The Warner house was willed to West Point and is now a national historic landmark.

Susan received greater literary fame in her lifetime than Anna. But Anna, who wrote many hymns for her Bible class, including "We Would See Jesus," "Jesus Bids Us Shine," and others, is remembered the world over for "Jesus Loves Me, This I Know."

> *Jesus loves me! this I know,*
> *For the Bible tells me so;*
> *Little ones to Him belong,*
> *They are weak, but He is strong.*
> *Yes, Jesus loves me,*
> *Yes, Jesus loves me,*
> *Yes, Jesus loves me,*
> *The Bible tells me so.*

43

Isaac Watts
1674–1748

Love so amazing, so divine,
Demands my soul, my life, my all.

ISAAC WATTS

Born in Southampton, England, Isaac Watts was the eldest of nine children. His mother was of Huguenot origin. His father, a scholarly man who taught his own children, was a respected nonconformist twice imprisoned for his religious beliefs. He also wrote poetry.

Isaac had a poetic mind from childhood. Once during family prayers the boy laughed out loud. When his parents questioned him about it, he said he had just seen a mouse run up the bell rope hanging by the fireplace, and he had made up a rhyme on the spot: "A mouse for want of better stairs/Ran up a rope to say his prayers."

Only five feet tall, Watts had a large head—made larger by a huge wig—and small piercing eyes. But he was known for his generosity, humility, and godliness. As a young man, he had proposed to a lovely lady. In refusing she responded, "I like the jewel but not the setting."

Books were Watts's chosen companions in his many times of illness, and he maintained an extensive correspondence. During one bout with ill health when he was thirty-eight, he was invited to spend a week on the estate of Sir Thomas Abney, his friend and admirer. As his health did not improve, the Abneys invited him to stay longer. He so endeared himself to the family that he remained for the rest of his life—thirty-six years!

Watts had a rich Christian background, and most of his hymns are paraphrases of the Bible. He had once complained to his father that the hymns sung at that time were so tuneless. His father smiled and suggested that he provide something better. So at the age of eighteen he wrote, "Behold the Glories of the Lamb." This was the birth of the English hymn. Watts created the model for English hymns just as Ambrose did for Latin hymns.

Watts's volume, *Hymns and Spiritual Songs*, published in 1707, was the first real hymnbook in the English language. Before this, only Psalms were sung in church, but he saw no reason why Christian praise should be confined, as Calvin insisted, to the actual language of the Bible. Watts sought to make it possible for God's people to sing His Word in the form of good poetry.

During the last thirty years of Watts's life, he was more or less an invalid. But in comfortable, happy surroundings he continued to use his brilliant mind to write hymns and books. Like Calvin, he had a powerful mind in a frail body, and like Calvin, his literary work was prodigious in spite of weakness and much illness.

Watts wrote more than six hundred hymns, as well as many books. His joyful hymns helped to prepare the way for the great revival under the Wesleys and Whitefield. He is also the founder of children's hymnody, producing the first hymnbook for children, *Divine Songs*.

Samuel Johnson said of Watts, "Few men have left behind such purity of character or such monuments of laborious piety." Hanging in Westminster Abbey is a tablet picturing Watts writing at a table while angels whisper songs in his ear. He was one of the most popular poets and preachers in England.

Three of his best-loved hymns are "Joy to the World, the Lord Is Come!" "When I Survey the Wondrous Cross," and "O God, Our Help in Ages Past."

> *Jesus shall reign where'er the sun*
> *Does his successive journeys run;*
> *His kingdom stretch from shore to shore,*
> *Till moons shall wax and wane no more.*

44

Charles Wesley
1707–1788

*If the succession of hymn writers can be
compared to a long range of hills, Wesley
is like a towering peak among them.*

ELSIE HOUGHTON

Generally people remember John Wesley as the preacher and Charles Wesley as the hymn writer; however, that is not totally correct. Charles was a good preacher also, but write hymns he did—over 6,000 of them. Obviously many are mediocre, but at his best he is unsurpassed. Certain of his hymns will not be forgotten while singing people are left in this world.

Charles was the eighteenth child of Susannah and Samuel Wesley. He was born several weeks before his time and appeared more dead than alive, but was carefully wrapped in warm wool. On the day he was supposed to be born, he opened his eyes and cried.

Then when he was only seventeen months old, another miracle occurred. His father, rector of Epworth, had several disgruntled members in his parish. One night these men set fire to the rectory. The baby survived because a maid courageously carried him out of the burning building in her arms.

The Wesley children were strictly home-schooled by their parents. Particularly, it was their remarkable mother who most strongly influenced their lives. Charles went to Oxford, like his brother John, and began to live a disciplined life there. He influenced some of his fellow students to join him, and the group became known as "Methodists."

Charles did not really become a Christian until he returned from a missionary trip to Georgia with his brother John in 1738. On the trip to the United States he met a Mr. Bray, whom Charles describes as "a poor, innocent mechanic who knows nothing but Christ." Later through Bray's sister, Mrs. Turner, he found the assurance of salvation he was seeking. As she spoke to him about Christ, he picked up his Bible and opened to: "He hath put a new song in my mouth, even praise unto our God" (Psalm 40:3). He was also greatly encouraged spiritually by reading Luther's *Commentary on Galatians* and through his contact with Count Zinzendorf.

After his conversion Charles spent much time visiting the inmates in Newgate Prison. He was particularly concerned for the criminals under sentence of death and spent many a night in their cells comforting and praying with them before their execution. This compassion often brought him into contact with the sordidness of life in the London of his day. Due to his sensitive, artistic nature, he frequently became depressed. Yet in these times he wrote some of his best hymns. His wife often accompanied him on his evangelistic journeys—a great encouragement to him.

Both Charles and John Wesley never tired of telling individuals the simple and direct message of God's mercy and how any life can be changed dramatically by accepting and believing the truth. They were indefatigable as field preachers.

Charles Wesley had the gift to express sublime truths in simple language. His hymns demonstrate this ability—"Jesus, Lover of My Soul," "Love Divine, All Loves Excelling," "Come, Thou Long Expected Jesus," "Hark, the Herald Angels Sing," and "Jesus Christ Is Risen Today." Filled with the great doctrines of the Trinity, the Incarnation, and the Resurrection, these hymns express the range of religious feeling.

Once Peter Bohler, one of Wesley's Moravian friends, said to him, "If I had one thousand tongues, I'd praise Christ with them all." These words went into Wesley's heart, and one year after his conversion he wrote:

> *O for a thousand tongues to sing*
> *My great Redeemer's praise,*
> *The glories of my God and King,*
> *The triumphs of His grace.*

The Methodist hymnody begun by John and Charles Wesley became one of the most powerful evangelizing influences on England. It was John who edited, organized, and published the endless flow of hymns from Charles. It was John Wesley who realized the importance of hymn singing in the work of evangelization; yet it was mainly Charles who provided hymns for the spread of Methodism and for the whole body of Christian churches in the following centuries.

Rejoice, the Lord is King:
Your Lord and King adore!
Rejoice, give thanks, and sing,
And triumph evermore:
Lift up your heart, Lift up your voice!
Rejoice, again I say, rejoice!

45

John Wesley
1703–1791

The world is my parish.

JOHN WESLEY

When John Wesley was five years old, the Epworth Rectory where the Wesley family lived caught fire. John was the last person to be rescued. Ever afterward his mother thought of him as "a brand plucked from the burning," and she prayed that she would be "more specially careful of the soul of this child." That was no easy task, as John's mother had had nineteen children in twenty years.

Susannah, an intelligent woman of deep piety, taught her children to read the Bible as soon as they were able to walk. Since her husband was never out of debt, Susannah had the responsibility of feeding her children physically and spiritually. Even as a mature man, John still sought her advice in important matters. A splendid result of her teaching was that he read widely throughout his life, although he called himself a man of one book, the Bible.

While at Oxford he became the leader of a small group of students, including his brother Charles and George Whitefield, who met for Bible study and prayer. Known as "The Holy Club," they taught a system of methods for living a Christian life and were derisively called "Methodists."

Sometime between 1735 and 1738 Wesley went as a missionary to the colony of Georgia in America. He thought he would find unspoiled children of nature who might open their hearts to the rules and methods of The Holy Club. Instead he found a world filled with rape, murder, and sin. His work there bore no fruit. As he wrote in his journal on the trip back to England, "It is upwards two years since I left my native country in order to teach the Georgian Indians the nature of Christianity, but what have I learned? Why, what I least of all suspected, that I, who went to America to convert others, was never converted myself . . ."

The trip back to England was stormy and dangerous. Wesley was deeply impressed by the calm faith of a group of passengers, Moravians from Austria, who sang hymns in the midst of the storm.

Soon after his return to London in 1738, John attended a Moravian meeting. As he listened to the reading of Martin Luther's preface to the book of Romans, his heart was "strangely warmed." Light suddenly dawned on his soul, and at last he found peace with God through Christ.

From that time on, John Wesley began preaching about the saving power of Christ by faith, a theme he emphasized for fifty years. Although he remained firmly Anglican, those churches closed their doors to his message. It was not long before he followed George Whitefield's example and began to hold outdoor meetings that attracted vast crowds. The preachers suffered much persecution and criticism, but the great evangelical revival had begun, and Methodism spread rapidly throughout England and the United States

John Wesley journeyed to Halle, Germany, shortly after his conversion in 1738 to learn more about Luther and the Pietists. There he met the Moravian leader, Count von Zinzendorf of Herrnhut, who encouraged him to translate some of the beautiful German hymns. The masterly translation of Count Zinzendorf's original verses, "Jesus, Thy Blood and Righteousness," came to us this way. Wesley understood the value of hymns that express the evangelical faith in simple language.

Possessing extraordinary energy and enthusiasm, Wesley often preached fifteen sermons a week. He traveled mostly on horseback—nearly 5,000 miles a year. While riding through the countryside, he wrote many of his books. He was one of the busiest men in England, usually getting up at 4 A.M. and never wasting a minute until retiring at 10 P.M.

John Wesley and George Whitefield led one of the greatest spiritual movements in the history of the Christian church. Their preaching ignited a great revival that possibly delivered England from a revolution like the one that tore France apart. A master of organization and intensely practical, Wesley achieved his mission to spread "Scriptural holiness." Although he received large sums of money for his publications—his spiritual autobiography *Journals* is a classic—Wesley gave all his money to charity and died without means. Surely he was one of the great Christians of all time.

Jesus, Thy blood and righteousness
My beauty are, my glorious dress;
'Midst flaming worlds, in these arrayed,
With joy shall I lift up my head.

46

John Greenleaf Whittier

1807–1892

Doing God's will as if it were my own,
Yet trusting not in mine,
but in His strength alone.

JOHN GREENLEAF WHITTIER

Whittier had few playmates his own age, but with good Quaker parents, relatives, and his brilliant sister "Lizzie," he had all the companionship he needed. Raised in extreme poverty, John worked hard as a farm boy and as a shoemaker. He was poor most of his life and never received a formal college education. But he loved to read and in the process educated himself. Also, Whittier was well instructed in the Bible at home, probably far better than he would have been taught at school.

At age fourteen, he discovered the writings of Robert Burns. In Burns, who wrote about farm life, John found one of his own kind. He began to write poetry. When his older sister Mary read these poems, she urged him to send one to a newspaper, but he was too shy. Taking matters into her own hands, she sent his best one to the editor of the *Newburyport Free Press*. The editor, later to become Whittier's lifelong friend, asked for more poems. He was so impressed with what he received that he rode to the Whittier farm to meet the poet. He found John on his hands and knees searching for eggs.

For some years Whittier had an extensive journalistic career working for various newspapers and was closely associated with the *Atlantic Monthly*. He became a successful journalist, editor, and poet—known for his sense of humor.

With the publication of his masterpiece, *Snow-Bound*, Whittier's national reputation as a writer was securely established. His poetry strikes a warm note of human sympathy that continues to appeal to each new generation of readers.

Whittier was deeply influenced by the great English poet John Milton, whose role as a leader in the cause of freedom and righteous living he sought to imitate. Both had strong faith in democracy, truth, and justice. Whittier said, "What is the benefit of great talents if they be not devoted to goodness?" So he bent his talents to bringing political change. Preeminently the poet of abolition, he condemned the hypocrisy of a nation founded on the ideals of freedom but allowing slavery. In writing a tribute to an editor of a newspaper, Whittier said, "He was one of those men who mold and shape the age in which they live." Whittier too fit that description.

He was one of the most deeply religious poets in American literature. His fervent love for God shone through all his work, especially his many hymns, of which the best-known is "Dear Lord and Father of Mankind." This beautiful hymn shows Whittier's grasp of the truth that one can only reach God through simplicity and sincerity.

Dear Lord and Father of mankind,
Forgive our foolish ways!
Reclothe us in our rightful mind,
In purer lives Thy service find,
In deeper reverence, praise.

47

Catherine Winkworth
1827–1878

Shakespeare, Leonardo da Vinci, Benjamin
Franklin, and Abraham Lincoln never saw a movie,
heard a radio, or looked at television. They had
"loneliness" and knew what to do with it. They were
not afraid of being lonely because they knew that was
when the creative mood in them would work.

CARL SANDBURG

Hymn singing as we know it today had its beginning in Germany, and the foremost translator from German into English was Catherine Winkworth. She had a special gift for preserving the spirit of the great German hymns while translating them. As Robin A. Leaver said in *Catherine Winkworth—The Influence of Her Translations on English Hymnody*, "She faithfully transplanted Germany's best hymns and made them bloom with fresh beauty in their new gardens."

Catherine Winkworth was not asked by anyone to translate hymns, nor did she receive an advance royalty from a publisher. Her translations were originally for her own personal devotional life. That they were printed later and highly thought of in her lifetime is wonderful, but I will always remember that her first intention was to praise the Lord in the privacy of her own room.

Quietly singing a hymn when we are tired, discouraged, or sad is extremely refreshing. Next to the Bible, a good hymnbook is a Christian's greatest devotional guide. When singing hymns in church, we often miss the meaning, but reading the words and singing them when alone brings fresh spiritual insight.

Catherine Winkworth was born in London and spent most of her life in the vicinity of Manchester. She was a bright child, but delicate, and suffered extended periods of illness. Having a great thirst for knowledge, she used her times of forced inactivity (due to sickness) to study and learn. Hers was a combination of rare ability and great knowledge, with a sympathetic refinement, and she was an expert linguist.

Both of her parents were Evangelical Christians. She was particularly close to her father, a kindly, devout, and sensitive man, fond of art and music. Her mother died when Catherine was quite young, and her father remarried. Much like Frances Ridley Havergal, she suffered greatly as the stepmother came between her and her father's affection.

Catherine grew up loving hymns and hymn singing, partly through the influence of her tutors. To one of these teachers, William Gaskell, Catherine attributed her thorough knowledge of English. Possibly she also gained linguistic skills from his wife, Elizabeth, who wrote the superb biography of Charlotte Brontë. Catherine was influenced by his Unitarian theology, but gradually she returned to the Evangelical position.

There were other people in Catherine's life who shared her love for hymns. She was a friend of the Brontë sisters. Anne, the youngest, was a hymn writer as well as a novelist. Catherine also had two hymn-singing uncles who were connected with Lady

Huntingdon's Chapel at Tunbridge Wells. She was probably familiar with Lady Huntingdon's hymnbook, a basic anthology of Evangelical hymnody.

Lady Huntingdon was one of the key figures of the Methodist revival. A brilliant noblewoman who was widowed in her thirties, she used her wealth and influence to sponsor preachers like George Whitefield and to sponsor hymnists and musicians. Understanding the value of hymn singing, Lady Huntingdon edited hymnals and even wrote melodies for use in the chapels she established.

Catherine Winkworth translated nearly four hundred texts by about one hundred and seventy authors. Her translations are the most widely used of any from the German language. John Julian said, "They have had more to do with the modern revival of the English use of German hymns than the versions of any other writer" (*A Dictionary of Hymnology*).

She had an "eye and ear" for the best of German hymns, and these are ranked with the classic English hymns of the nineteenth century. Her hymn translations such as "How Brightly Beams the Morning Star," "Wake, Awake for Night Is Flying," "If Thou But Suffer God to Guide Thee," "Jesus, Priceless Treasure," "All Glory Be to God on High," and many others are to be found in every good hymnbook. Some of these hymn tunes are the basis of many of the glorious Bach chorales.

The hymn sung by the congregation during worship was born with the Reformation under Luther. Philip Schaff in his *History of the Christian Church* said, "To Luther belongs the extraordinary merit of having given to the German people in their own tongue the Bible, the Catechism, and the hymnbook, so that God might speak *directly* to them in His words, and that they might *directly* answer Him in their songs."

It is enlightening to trace the chain of influence and relationships God used to nurture His church with music back one step further. Ursula Cotta and her husband heard Martin Luther singing in the cold streets of Eisenach to earn money for his education. Observing how fragile and needy he was, they invited him to live with them. In the culturally rich atmosphere of their home, Luther received a new thirst for knowledge and encouragement to sing and play the lute. Music under Luther's influence became a vital force in the spread of the Reformation.

In 1855 Winkworth's book, *Lyra Germanica* (translations of German chorales), was published and was well received by the public. Another of her excellent books is *Christian Singers of Germany*. Even though she first translated some of the hymns to encourage herself, she soon began to realize what jewels she had. Her chief aim was to acquaint English and American churches with the wealth of German hymns.

When able, she promoted the rights of women to be educated, and she helped establish a college in Bristol where women had equal opportunity to attend classes along with men.

Though tired and unwell in the years between 1872 and 1875, Catherine made a number of visits to France and Germany. On one of these trips she was a delegate to the Congress of Women in Darmstadt. Again she went to France in 1878 to look after an invalid nephew. On her way to Mornex in Savoy, she suffered a heart attack and died at the age of fifty-one in the village of Monnetier. There she is buried, and on her tomb these words are engraved: *"Blessed are the pure in heart, For they shall see God."*

It was not easy for us to find Monnetier (the books about Miss Winkworth all said that it was near Geneva). Even two French policemen we asked did not know where it was, but finally we saw a small sign and kept going up and up and around and around until we arrived in the village and were directed to the cemetery. A pleasant French lady showed us the grave. On the tomb is a beautifully carved cross.

Through her translations Catherine Winkworth has enabled the German hymns to be known, sung, and loved, not only in England, but throughout the world. Wherever English hymns are sung, her translations will always be among them.

> *Now thank we all our God*
> *With heart and hands and voices!*
> *Who wondrous things hath done,*
> *In Whom His world rejoices;*
> *Who from our mothers' arms*
> *Hath blessed us on our way*
> *With countless gifts of love;*
> *And still is ours today.*

MARTIN RINKART (WORDS),
CATHERINE WINKWORTH (TRANSLATOR)

Writers Remembered
for a Single Hymn

If your heart is set on a
certain goal in life,
and you cannot achieve it,
do something else.

BETTY CARLSON

Some hymn writers are known for only one hymn. In this chapter we speak briefly about several of these women. They surely did not despise the day of small things. They also understood what Zechariah said in 4:6, "'Not by might nor by power, but by my Spirit,' says the Lord Almighty."

Phoebe Cary
(1824–1871)

"One Sweetly Solemn Thought"

Phoebe was born on a farm in Ohio and was well acquainted with poverty in her youth. Later she moved to New York and became involved in literary pursuits at the same time her sister

Elizabeth Prentiss was writing her hymns and books. Phoebe's life was enriched by a friendship with John Greenleaf Whittier, the Quaker poet and hymn writer.

In her more creative years, Phoebe Cary said, "I have cried in the streets because I was poor, and so the poor always seem nearer to me than the rich."

When she died, her hymn "One Sweetly Solemn Thought" was sung at her funeral.

> *One sweetly solemn thought*
> *Comes to me o'er and o'er;*
> *I am nearer my home today*
> *Than I ever have been before.*

Emily Steele Elliott
(1836–1897)

"Thou Didst Leave Thy Throne"

Emily Steele Elliott, the niece of Charlotte Elliott, was born in Brighton, England. Her father was a rector, and most of her hymns were written for his church services. Sometimes people think poets and writers live in "another world." To a certain extent they do! But one of the best ways to help them get on with all the ideas moving in their minds is to commission a work for a specific occasion.

Emily was often asked to write hymns for functions at the

church. As we said in our book on composers, *The Gift of Music*, Bach wrote a great deal of his music because the church where he was organist needed chorales, cantatas, organ works, etc. for the coming week.

The text for this Christmas hymn is Luke 2:7, "Because there was no room for them in the inn."

> *Thou didst leave Thy throne and Thy kingly crown,*
> *When Thou camest to earth for me;*
> *But in Bethlehem's home was there found no room*
> *For Thy holy Nativity.*
> *Oh, come to my heart, Lord Jesus!*
> *There is room in my heart for Thee.*

Dorothy F. Gurney
(1858–1932)

"O Perfect Love"

This hymn is considered by some to be the finest and most impressive wedding hymn ever written. It was sung at Jane's mother's wedding, and Jane herself has sung it at various weddings of friends. The London *Times* observed upon Dorothy Gurney's death that thousands of people at thousands of weddings must have sung, or heard sung "O Perfect Love" without knowing that Mrs. Gurney wrote it. To her it was always a matter of amused regret that she did not get a royalty for each performance.

> *O perfect Love, all human thought transcending,*
> *Lowly we kneel in prayer before Thy throne,*
> *That theirs may be the love that knows no ending,*
> *Whom Thou for evermore dost join in one.*

Julia H. Johnston
(1849–1919)

"Marvelous Grace of Our Loving Lord"

Julia Johnston was a Christian educator, writer, and hymnist. She served as a Sunday school superintendent for over forty years and was president of the Church Missionary Society for twenty years. She wrote several hundred hymns, but only this hymn is regularly sung in churches.

> *Marvelous grace of our loving Lord,*
> *Grace that exceeds our sin and our guilt,*
> *Yonder on Calvary's mount outpoured,*
> *There where the blood of the Lamb was spilt.*
> *Grace, grace, God's grace,*
> *Grace that will pardon and cleanse within;*
> *Grace, grace, God's grace,*
> *Grace that is greater than all our sin.*

Civilla D. Martin

(1867–1948)

"His Eye Is on the Sparrow"

Civilla Martin and her husband were visiting friends, the Doolittles, in Elmira, New York. Both Mr. and Mrs. Doolittle were confined to wheelchairs. In spite of handicaps, they were courageous and cheerful. Greatly impressed by the saintly couple, Dr. Martin commented on their joy. Mrs. Doolittle looked at the visitors and said simply, "His eye is on the sparrow, and I know He watches me."

Before the day ended, Mrs. Martin used this sentence in one of the most touching of hymns. Gospel singer Ethel Waters often sang "His Eye Is on the Sparrow" at Billy Graham Crusades.

Why should I feel discouraged,
Why should the shadows come,
Why should my heart be lonely
and long for heav'n and home,
When Jesus is my portion?
My constant friend is He:
His eye is on the sparrow,
and I know He watches me;
His eye is on the sparrow,
and I know He watches me.

Adelaide A. Pollard

(1862–1934)

"Have Thine Own Way, Lord"

Adelaide Pollard possessed a talent for writing and produced many articles and some hymns. Interested in evangelism, she traveled widely, speaking to groups and at various church gatherings.

Once as she sat in a prayer meeting, she was so depressed she could hardly concentrate on what was being said. She longed to go to Africa as a missionary, but was unable to raise the necessary funds.

Suddenly this thought came to her, *It's all right, Lord! It doesn't matter what You bring into our lives. Just have Your own way with us.* Gradually she felt the burden lift, and in her submission to the will of God, she found peace again.

Later, after meditating on Jeremiah 18:3, 4, she wrote her hymn. In God's own time, He did allow her to go as an evangelist to Africa.

This frail, little woman was so modest that her hymns were signed only with her initials. "Have Thine Own Way, Lord" is Adelaide Pollard's only hymn to stand the test of time, and it has become a favorite throughout the Christian world.

> *Have Thine own way, Lord!*
> *Have Thine own way!*
> *Thou art the Potter; I am the clay.*
> *Mold me and make me after Thy will,*
> *While I am waiting, yielded and still.*

Mary Ann Thomson
(1834–1923)

"O Zion Haste"

Mary Ann was born in London. Later she came to America where she married John Thomson, the first librarian of the Free Library in Philadelphia. A gifted writer, she was particularly fond of composing hymns. At a time of deep anxiety due to the critical illness of one of her children, she was inspired to write "O Zion Haste." It has become a great missionary hymn.

> O Zion, haste, thy mission high fulfilling,
> To tell to all the world that God is Light,
> That He who made all nations is not willing
> One soul should perish, lost in shades of night.
> Publish glad tidings; Tidings of peace;
> Tidings of Jesus, Redemption and release.

Postlude

At the Saturday night buffets at Chalet Chesalet, we always sing at the conclusion of the meals. One time some of us were talking about our favorite hymns. Several in the group answered immediately which hymn they liked best. It has taken me a few years to recognize what my favorites are.

Many of you reading this book also have certain favorite contemporary hymns that you sing at various meetings and church services. Nevertheless, we will not know until we reach heaven which of our favorites have enduring quality. Hymns, as well as all art, need to be tested by time. Most hymns are sung for a while and then pass into oblivion. Those based on Scripture are generally the most enduring.

In his book *Greatness in Music*, Alfred Einstein made this remarkable statement: "Artistic greatness is both more permanent and universal than historical greatness." Jane commented on this remark in *The Gift of Music:* "Remembering that the Christian Church from the first made use of the arts, we should be challenged to have them take their proper place again. . . . The arts in a Christian framework are an act of worship, and we should be willing to work on them, striving to make artistic statements worthy of the Lord in whom we believe."

A Note
About the Authors

Jane Stuart Smith graduated in liberal arts from Stuart Hall and Hollins College in Virginia. She studied further at the Juilliard School of Music in New York and the Tanglewood Festival School of Music in Massachusetts. Her chief voice teacher was Maestro Ettore Verna. As a dramatic soprano, Miss Smith has sung in major opera houses in Europe and America. At present she lives in Switzerland where she is a member and the international secretary of L'Abri Fellowship. She lectures on art, literature, and music. In her many years in Huemoz, she has originated and participated in numerous art and music festivals, has given concerts in the United States, Canada, and Europe with the L'Abri Ensemble, and has made a variety of musical recordings.

Betty Carlson has a B.A. from Grinnell College and an M.S. from Oregon State College. She has also studied at the Conservatory of Music in Lausanne, Switzerland. Among the various books she has written are *The Unhurried Chase, A New Song from L'Abri* (which tells how Jane came from the opera world to Huemoz), *No One's Perfect,* and *Reflections from a Small Chalet.* She is a volunteer worker at L'Abri.

Composers
in Chronological Order

340–397   Ambrose of Milan

1090–1153 Bernard of Clairvaux

1483–1546 Martin Luther

1593–1633 George Herbert

1608–1674 John Milton

1628–1688 John Bunyan

1637–1711 Thomas Ken

1672–1719 Joseph Addison

1674–1748 Isaac Watts

1702–1751 Philip Doddridge

1703–1791 John Wesley

1707–1788 Charles Wesley

1725–1807 John Newton

1731–1800 William Cowper

1740–1817 John Fawcett

1740–1778 Augustus M. Toplady

1752–1817 Timothy Dwight

1771–1854 James Montgomery

1783–1826 Reginald Heber

1789–1871   Charlotte Elliott

1792–1872   Lowell Mason

1793–1847   Henry F. Lyte

1805–1848   Sarah Flower Adams

1807–1892   John Greenleaf Whittier

1808–1889   Horatius Bonar

1808–1887   Ray Palmer

1810–1871   Henry Alford

1811–1896   Harriet Beecher Stowe

1813–1897   Jane L. Borthwick

1813–1906   Jemima Luke

1818–1866   John Mason Neale

1818–1878   Elizabeth P. Prentiss

1819–1910   Julia Ward Howe

1819–1886   Joseph Scriven

1820–1915   Fanny J. Crosby

1820–1915   Anna Bartlett Warner

1823–1895   Cecil Frances Alexander

1823–1897   William W. How

1823–1907   Sara Borthwick Findlater

1824–1871   Pheobe Cary

1827–1878   Catherine Winkworth

1830–1869   Elizabeth Clephane

1830–1894   Christina Rossetti

1832–1903   Lina Sandell

1834–1911   A. Catherine Hankey

1834–1923   Mary Ann Thomson

1835–1893   Phillips Brooks

1835–1918   Annie S. Hawks

1836–1897   Emily Steele Elliott

1836–1879   Frances Ridley Havergal

1841–1913   Mary A. Lathbury

1849–1919   Julia H. Johnston

1858–1932   Dorothy F. Gurney

1859–1929   Katherine Lee Bates

1862–1934   Adelaide A. Pollard

1867–1948   Civilla D. Martin

Select
Bibliography

Benson, Louis F. *The Hymnody of the Christian Church*. Richmond, VA: John Knox Press, 1956.

Brown and Butterworth. *The Story of the Hymns and Tunes*. Grand Rapids: Zondervan Publishing House.

Christian Praise. Downers Grove, IL: Inter-Varsity Press, 1957.

Colquhoun, Frank. *Hymns That Live*. London: Hodder and Stoughton, 1980.

Deen, Edith. *Great Women of the Christian Faith*. New York: Harper and Brothers Publishers, 1959.

Fountain, David. *Isaac Watts Remembered*. Worthing, England: Brown and Son, Ltd., 1974.

Grierson, Janet. *Frances Ridley Havergal*. Worchester, England: The Havergal Society, 1979.

Halleck, Reuben P. *History of English Literature*. New York: American Book Company, 1900.

Hammack, Mary L. *A Dictionary of Women in Church History*. Chicago: Moody Press, 1984.

Houghton, Elsie. *Christian Hymn Writers*. Worcestor: Evangelical Press of Wales, 1982.

Jackson, Samuel M., ed. *The New Schaff-Herzog Encyclopedia of Religious Knowledge*. Grand Rapids: Baker Book House, 1953.

Johnson, Samuel. *Lives of the English Poets*. New York: Dutton, 1925.

Julian, John. *A Dictionary of Hymnology*. New York: Dover Publications, Inc., 1957.

Knapp, Christopher. *Who Wrote Our Hymns?* Oak Park, IL: Bible Truth Publishers, 1925.

Leaver, Robin A. *Catherine Winkworth—The Influence of Her Translations on English Hymnody.* St. Louis, MO: Concordia Publishing House, 1978.

Osbeck, Kenneth W. *101 Hymn Stories.* Grand Rapids: Kregel Publications, 1982.

Rudin, Cecilia Margaret. *Stories of Hymns We Love.* Chicago: John Rudin and Co., Inc., 1955.

Ruffin, Bernard. *Fanny Crosby.* New York: United Church Press, 1976.

Ryden, E. E. *The Story of Christian Hymnody.* Rock Island, IL: Augustana Press, 1959.

Thomas, Eleanor Walter. *Christina Georgina Rossetti.* New York: Columbia University Press, 1931.

Thomas, R. S. *A Choice of George Herbert's Verse.* London: Faber and Faber, 1967.

Trinity Hymnal. Philadelphia: Great Commission Publications, 1962.

Winkworth, Catherine. *Christian Singers of Germany.* London: Macmillan and Co. Publishers, 1869.

Index to
Hymn Titles